GOD'S OWN
ENTREPRENEURS

The Success Secrets of 21 Entrepreneurs from Kerala

R ROSHAN

ISBN 979-8-88629-970-0

CONTENTS

ABOUT THE AUTHOR

R.Roshan is a business journalist with more than 15 years of experience, and is an author of several books. He began his business journalism career in 2004. Currently, he oversees the business news division of Mathrubhumi, a leading Malayalam daily.

He has authored Malayalam books titled 'Swarnathil Engane Nikshepikkam' (How to Invest in Gold), 'Ohari Nikshepam Ariyendathellam' (All You Need to Know About Investing in Stock Market), 'Startup: Thudangam Puthusamrambhangal' (Startup: Let's Start New Ventures), and Vijayapathakal (Success Paths).

He is also a startup evangelist, who is passionate about emerging businesses. Roshan was honoured by the Kerala Startup Mission in 2022. And in 2021, he received the Bisgate Excellence Award for the best business journalist.

He lives in Kochi and tweets at @rroshandotcom

FOREWARD

Kerala has a deep history of entrepreneurship that dates back to the time when this narrow strip of land on the west coast of India started trading in spices with Arabs and later with the Portuguese. Since time immemorial, it has produced some excellent and bold entrepreneurs, many of whose names are lost to the sands of time.

Today, we live in a world where becoming an entrepreneur is easier than it has ever been. Better access to capital, resources, exposure and to markets that are less constrained by boundaries, have made this a golden age of entrepreneurship.

We are also fortunate that today's entrepreneurial journeys are being increasingly well chronicled. Roshan in his fascinating book 'God's Own Entrepreneurs' writes about 21 entrepreneurs from Kerala who created large global businesses. He records their less-known stories, failures, and eventual triumphs in creating large conglomerates. While the reader will learn that they all come from different businesses ranging from construction, gold trading, hotels, healthcare, and retail to tech, there are some consistent themes that mark their rise - remarkable persistence, creativity, and a determined refusal to accept the status quo. Political or economic boundaries did not inhibit them as they conceived or ran their businesses.

Whether it's M.A.Yusuff Ali who built a giant retail business on foreign shores or Kris Gopalakrishnan and S.D.Shibulal, who built a tech conglomerate out of India taking on global giants, or Byju Raveendran's audacious journey of building the world's most valuable ed-tech company, each of these stories is unique. The book takes us deeper into their motivations, their personal philosophies, what made them venture into the businesses they eventually shone in, and how they managed to scale heights in those businesses. In addition to creating large enterprises, they have created tens of thousands of jobs.

Roshan draws from his rich experience as a journalist and an ardent observer of the start-up ecosystem in telling us the stories of these different individuals with varied backgrounds connected only by that invisible thread we call "entrepreneurial spirit."

As a Malayali starting on an entrepreneurial adventure after nearly 20 years of corporate life, this book is fascinating, revealing, and insightful for me. These are just 21 names, but many more stories of entrepreneurs from the state are waiting to be told. Let us look up to Roshan for those stories to be told.

– Parry Ravindranathan

Former Managing Director – International, Bloomberg

FOREWARD

Very rarely do we have a book that chronicles inspiring entrepreneurship stories from Kerala. 'God's Own Entrepreneurs', by R. Roshan is such a book. It can best be described as concise yet detailed. There is more useful information packed into its 21 mini-bios/chapters than seen in most books three times its size. Thus, it gives me great pleasure to write this foreword.

I have been following Roshan's work since the beginning of my entrepreneurship journey in India. I have also witnessed the unconditional support of Roshan to the entrepreneurs from Kerala. After reading the manuscript, I can say that Roshan's pure intention of speaking about Kerala's economic growth story is evident in 'God's Own Entrepreneurs.'

The core purpose of my company, Hurun Report, is to speak about Indian stories through the eyes of the entrepreneurs and companies that feature in the list. Through Hurun Research, we mainly identify these stories, "quantify" and celebrate them. 'God's Own Entrepreneurs' goes one level deeper and gives another dimension to the reader to decipher why these stories have to be celebrated. For instance, in the very first chapter on M.A. Yusuff Ali, who has been the richest Keralite in the Hurun India Rich List for almost a decade, Roshan mentions how Mr. Yusuff Ali withstood the Gulf war to earn the respect of UAE and build one of the most valuable businesses there. Such detailing in some stories imparted critical new info and insight to me which is the biggest highlight of the book.

I am also an active angel investor and have predominantly backed companies that are founded by Malayalis. Being active in the angel investment space, I appreciate the role played by Roshan in speaking about the growth stories of Kerala startups. Connecting the dots, I gather from reading 'God's Own Entrepreneurs' that Roshan has one audience in his mind – future Malayali entrepreneurs. This book will delight their palate.

And lastly, the book gives a bird's eye view into the early life of some of the business stalwarts from Kerala. Every story is a case study and will serve as an inspiration to entrepreneurs. They show, despite limitations, one can create wealth using sheer grit and perseverance.

To summarise, 'God's Own Entrepreneurs' is a book that should be on the desks of all entrepreneurs, government officials, startups and senior professionals. I am sure you will enjoy reading the same as I did.

– Anas Rahman Junaid

Founder and Managing Director, Hurun India

PREFACE

Being a business journalist, I often get to closely interact with India's top industrialists and professionals. These interactions have always been exciting for two reasons: one, the possibility of landing a scoop, and second, I get a chance to learn new things from these great people who constantly inspire the wannabe entrepreneur in me to set my own moon shots.

My interest in journalism and entrepreneurship led me to opt for journalism for my higher studies as I believed it would help me understand both areas deeply. When I started my career as a business journalist, I paid special attention to preparing interviews and news that cater to aspiring entrepreneurs, which was a learning process for me too. Some years ago, I had the fortune of asking Infosys founder N.R. Narayana Murthy, when he was in Kochi, what are the must-have qualities for an aspiring entrepreneur. This is what he said: "Never take the entrepreneurial road half-heartedly. Try your best to turn your idea into a startup. You should also have deep knowledge about the area in which you are planning to launch your venture". Adi Godrej, head of the Godrej Group, one of the biggest business houses in India, also told me once about the importance of learning as you grow a business.

Later, close interactions with prominent Malayali businessmen further strengthened my belief in learning the ropes and preparing the ground before launching any business. Their journey to success was never a cakewalk as they had to overcome many challenges and setbacks on the path. I realised that their success stories needed to be celebrated along with the stories of startups the world looks up to for inspiration. However, unlike the Indian communities of Parsis, Marwaris, Jains, Chettiyars, and Khatris who are known for their business acumen, Malayalis, as a community, have not been lauded for their entrepreneurial spirit.

One of the reasons could be, in the beginning, Malayali entrepreneurs started their businesses abroad, the first destination being Ceylon, now Sri Lanka, for historical and geographical reasons. When Vasco da Gama landed in Calicut in 1498 from Europe, it set the stage for the launch of the colonial era in India. However, it also gave Malayalis exposure to the world outside. Trade interactions with the Chinese, the Portuguese, the Dutch and Arabs also sowed the seeds of entrepreneurship in Malayalis' minds, from where they took off.

The famous Malayali migration to the Gulf in the 1970s marked the beginning of the unparalleled entrepreneurial journey of the community. Malayalis scripted phenomenal success stories there and created wealth that their older generations could not dream of. It eventually inspired their friends and relatives back home to move to Gulf countries to launch their own ventures. They also launched businesses in their home state, creating job opportunities. Now, in a more connected world, Malayalis are spread across the globe with entrepreneurs among them venturing into sectors as diverse as tourism, hospitality, FMCG, retail, construction, spices sector, healthcare, and technology besides startups, registering unique success stories.

I was fortunate enough to meet many of these entrepreneurs and engage in long conversations with them personally and as part of my job. No management school in the world can teach you the wealth of knowledge these geniuses possess, which they gained through their unique journeys. In fact, the encouragement from many of my well-wishers and friends to share the invaluable wisdom of Malayali entrepreneurs with the world prompted me to write this book.

I hope 'God's Own Entrepreneurs' will help not only those who aspire to become entrepreneurs but also those who failed to succeed as entrepreneurs, to understand Malayalis and their entrepreneurial culture from close quarters. It will equally benefit the management students and faculties when they turn the pages to find that most of the management theories were applied successfully by these entrepreneurs in their businesses.

There are other Malayali business tycoons not featured in this book. In that sense, the book is not complete. I am optimistic that I can share their stories too with readers in another book. All stories in this book are equally important and riveting and all pages are unique having equal relevance. I hope readers will be able to draw a lot of inspiration from the book and expand their minds to explore new horizons in their life.

– R. Roshan

1

THE HUMBLE ROAD TO GREATNESS

M.A.Yusuff Ali was born on November 15, 1955, to Abdul Kader and Safia at Musaliyam Veettil in the tiny village of Nattika, Thrissur. As a young man, Yusuff Ali was keen on becoming a lawyer, but an apple never falls far from the tree. The Thrissur Nattika Musaliyam family were traditional merchants and greatly influenced by his family, Yusuff Ali toed the same line. Little Yusuff grew up under the watchful eyes of his grandfather, learning the values of humility and staying connected to his roots. His father and uncles ran a grocery store in Ahmedabad. After completing his schooling with Nattika Mappila Lower Primary School, Government Fisheries School, and St. Xavier's English Medium School Karanchira, the young Yusuff Ali moved to Ahmedabad to join the business.

He picked up the business fundamentals at the MK Brothers General Store with guidance from his family members. He was sure that he wouldn't want to end up running the store and living an average life. His dreams were far bigger than what the small store could hold. Promptly he secured a Diploma in Business.

It was the time when Malayalis, weaving dreams of a secure and better future, had begun to set sail for the Gulf. Yusuff Ali, only 17, spent many a night in his tiny quarters at Ahmedabad dreaming of a life in the Gulf. He was determined to pursue his dreams. In between attending to the business at the store and other errands, Yusuff managed to secure his passport. Finally, with hopes galore, he boarded the ship Dumra from Mumbai on December 26, 1973. He counted the hours and saw nights slowly turning into days, yet his dreams burnt bright all the while.

At last, the ship anchored at Port Rashid in Dubai on 31st December. His father's younger brother M.K.Abdullah, running a grocery business there, received him at the port. The drive from Dubai to Abu Dhabi took more than six hours, and the desert he saw was in stark contrast to what he visualised in his dreams. As he started living, Yusuff Ali could find even water and light were scarce there. With temperature scorching at more than 50 degrees, he had his exhausted sleeps on the terrace. But all these extreme conditions did not deter the young entrepreneur from chasing his dreams; on the contrary, they made him more resolute.

M.A.Yusuff Ali with the Prime Minister of India, Narendra Modi

WHEN LIFE GIVES YOU LEMONS…

Soon he started learning more about business by observing his customers and their demands. The efforts that he put in at the store led him further up the ladder. When he saw others importing grains and food supplies in large quantities and selling them at a considerable margin, he began to study the many possibilities it offered. He, too, began to import food products from various countries. He kept exploring new opportunities in sales.

In the first half of the 80s, he travelled to Australia, Singapore and Hong Kong, and came across large supermarkets where everything was available under one roof. The prospects that were on offer were incredibly vast! Yusuff Ali thought about introducing such modern supermarkets in the Gulf and soon opened one in 1989. Following its success, he kickstarted work on opening a large department store on Airport Road in Abu Dhabi. Yusuff Ali was firm on giving Abu Dhabi its biggest shopping experience yet.

But disaster struck so soon in 1990. The Gulf War broke out when work on the store entered its final stage with the inaugural day close by. It was a bolt from the blue for Yusuff Ali, who had spent his entire savings as a capital investment on the department store. He could see everybody fleeing the country with whatever they could hold in their hands. However, Yusuff Ali was not prepared to leave the country that had raised him thus far. He decided that he would open the supermarket, come what may. Thus, the first LuLu department store was inaugurated. The slogan in its advertisement read: 'I have faith in this country.'

The sheer boldness of his move grabbed the attention of the entire nation. When the news reached Sheikh Zayed bin Sultan Al Nahyan, the ruler of the UAE, he summoned Yusuff Ali to the palace. The Sheikh asked him how he mustered the courage to begin a new venture when everybody else was fleeing for their lives. His reply was straight: "I made all this from your country. My conscience doesn't allow me to leave when the country is going through a crisis. As long as you are the ruler, I am sure that nothing will happen to this country." The Sheikh embraced Yusuff Ali upon hearing these words. There began the success of MA Yusuff Ali, the entrepreneur.

The royal family gifted land for a number of his projects, including around 40 acres to build Mushrif Mall in Abu Dhabi. A plot worth Rs. 600 crores at Abu Dhabi's City Centre, where Yusuff Ali built a house, was also a gift from the royal family. He believes that the country has endowed him with immense fortune for the work that he put in over four-and-a-half decades.

M.A.Yusuff Ali with Sheikh Zayed bin Sultan Al Nahyan, UAE's Father of Nation

It has been a rollercoaster ride for the entrepreneur. During the war, ports in many countries, including Jordan, remained closed to prevent people from leaving. That was when Yusuff Ali waited for a shipment of food products at the Jordanian port from India. The port shut down when the cargo vessel had almost reached Jordan. Yusuff Ali waited for 21 days to unload the shipment but to no avail. Meanwhile, the war led to a famine in the UAE. Finally, Yusuff Ali travelled to Jordan, spoke with the army, and successfully unloaded the goods. If he had been unsuccessful, he would have lost crores of rupees. But the universe conspired against all odds to fulfil his dreams. He went to Mecca to perform Umrah and pay thanks to the Almighty. Similar challenges arose many times later too. But the optimist in Yusuff Ali, the entrepreneur, never let them weaken him. He turned all such challenges into opportunities.

HYPER TRENDSETTER

The 90s marked the upward journey of the LuLu network. What began with a small grocery store soon grew into supermarkets, department stores, hypermarkets, and malls offering an international shopping experience. Today, the LuLu network has more than 215 hypermarkets in the UAE, Bahrain, Kuwait, Oman, Qatar, Saudi Arabia, Egypt, India, Malaysia, and Indonesia, and more than a dozen shopping malls in various parts of the Gulf. With LuLu Mall opening at Edapally, Kochi, in March 2013, the company announced its presence in the Indian retail space as well.

Yusuff Ali always held his grandfather's teachings close to his heart. So, keen on helping prosper his homeland, he launched the LuLu Convention Centre in Thrissur. A shopping mall at Akkulam in Thiruvananthapuram is among his latest gifts to his home state. He has realised India's largest convention centre at Bolgatty in Kochi, which rubs shoulders with the Grand Hyatt Hotel, another monolith project he has undertaken. At Infopark Kochi stands LuLu Cyber Tower, the tallest IT tower in Kerala.

Apart from Kerala, malls and hypermarkets are now coming up in Uttar Pradesh, Karnataka, Tamil Nadu etc. spreading the LuLu footprint. Today, LuLu has a formidable presence in the retail sector, both offline and online. The LuLu Group has also established itself in the wholesale, food processing, export-import, shipping, IT, hotel, and travel-tourism sectors. In short, M.A. Yusuff Ali literally took the saying, 'the world is your oyster,' to his heart. His persistence in turning even the worst situations to his favour enabled him to rise to unimaginable heights.

But an emperor is nothing without the support of his retinue. The LuLu Group employs more than 56,000 people from around 37 countries. Among them, more than 25,000 are Keralites. Yusuff Ali says that being able to support so many families are what gives him the greatest contentment. To world leaders, business magnates, and employees, he is 'Yusuff Bhai', as Yusuff Ali does not like to be called 'Sir'. Most of the employees have been recruited by Yusuff Ali himself.

A report by global consultancy firm Deloitte notes that LuLu is one of the world's top ten fastest-growing retail chains. Yusuff Ali's acquisition of a stake in the East India Company, owned by the British who once ruled India, and his purchase of the Great Scotland Yard Hotel, previously the headquarters of the UK Metropolitan Police, caught global media attention.

Whatever he is to his employees, the world, and the media, at home, he is the same humble man who had left his village with dreams of making it big one day. His family consists of his doting wife Shabira and loving daughters Shabeena, Shafeena, and Shifa. He shares a very close relationship with his sons-in-law Dr. V.P. Shamsheer, Adeeb Ahamed, and Sharoon Shamsuddin. Currently, Shafeena is the CEO of Tables Food Company, Dr. Shamsheer is the Managing Director of VPS Healthcare, Adeeb Ahamed is the CEO of LuLu Financial Group, and Sharoon Shamsuddin, the CEO of ISYX Technologies.

The lessons that Yusuff Ali learned from decades of life as an entrepreneur are many. He is always keen on defending his values. His grandfather used to tell him that when one scales greater heights, they should not think that others are beneath them, then their downfall will begin. Yusuff Ali has always believed in giving a leg up to those around him because of his remarkable upbringing. He says: "The Prophet (Peace Be Upon Him) was a merchant. The Prophet has imparted, through conduct, lessons on how and when to trade and the ethics to follow while doing so. As a believer, I have tried to walk in the path of the Prophet. I meet a lot of businessmen from around the world. I ask them about their experiences too." Yusuff Ali has this advice to new entrepreneurs: "Failure happens when a business is started without identifying the market. Production should start only after identifying a point of retail."

His story inspires young geniuses who have an insatiable thirst to achieve success. His story teaches one of the essential things in life: "No matter where you are in life, humility powers a positive mindset in you. Regardless of difficult times, appreciate the people who have contributed their time and energy to help you reach the zenith."

M.A. YUSUFF ALI

What motivates one to strive for greatness? What prompts one to keep moving despite facing setbacks? How do people spot something that burns so deep within as desire that they then realize with all their efforts? The answer is different for different people. The paths to success are myriad. Some find their true calling after facing several washouts. Some are pushed towards it by unforeseen events. But there are a fortunate few who find themselves being handheld towards it by their families. Musaliyam Veettil Abdul Kader Yusuff Ali, better known as M.A.Yusuff Ali, has such a tale to tell. He went on to become the founder and Chairman of LuLu Group, one of the fastest-growing retail chains in the world.

He was at the 589th position on the Global Rich List-2021 of Forbes and has consistently been the richest Malayali in the Hurun India Rich List for some time. Yusuff Ali is recipient of numerous awards in India and abroad. He was awarded the Pravasi Bharatiya Samman in 2005 and the Padma Shri in 2008. He has also won the highest civilian honour of Bahrain and Abu Dhabi, bestowed on him by the rulers themselves.

Yusuff Ali is the first expatriate to become a member of the Abu Dhabi Chamber of Commerce and Industry (ADCCI) Board of Directors. He is the only non-Arab to be in the Director Board of this prestigious body for a record four times in a row. Currently, he is the Vice-Chairman of ADCCI appointed by H.H. Sheikh Mohammed Bin Zayed Al Nahyan, Crown Prince and Deputy Supreme Commander of the UAE Armed Forces. He is also the Vice-Chairman of NORKA Roots and a member of the Board of Directors of Cochin and Kannur airport companies.

2

A STELLAR RISE

Kollam, since the 1st century AD, has been recorded in history as a South Indian merchant town that always attracted businessmen, tradesmen, religious missionaries, and emperors. And this town served as the perfect place to nurture unfailing business instincts and strict work ethics in a young Ravi Pillai.

Being born into a well-respected agricultural family in Kollam, Kerala, meant that young Ravi Pillai was introduced to farming at a very young age. While others would've enjoyed the luxury of growing up in an affluent family, Pillai worked along with the farmers, the coir weavers, and others in the area. He had noticed the difficulties and tragedies in their lives, even at such a young age. And this understanding gave him the conviction to contribute to society when he eventually made a fortune in business.

Highly entrepreneurial right from childhood, the young man started a monthly chit fund during his college days, making much more than pocket money from it. While pursuing his MBA in Kochi, his friends suggested he'd be successful if he started his own business venture there. Thus, the young Ravi Pillai, with his youthful enthusiasm and a twinkle in his eye, launched his first business endeavour, securing contracts with industrial organizations like Fertilizers and Chemicals Travancore Limited (FACT), Cochin Refineries, and Hindustan Newsprint Limited. He also faced his first setback in his entrepreneurial life when the local workforce went on a strike, not driven by any ideological issues, but more by their parochial attitude towards an out-of-towner who was working hard towards business success. To the young man, this meant the time had come to take bigger strides, to pave his way through the big leaps.

Before the 1980s, the Middle East was in a predictable colonial hangover, and you had to be either American or European to receive respect or job contracts. The Koreans and the Japanese were revered for their knowledge and work ethics, but Indians generally held a reputation for being sluggish and unreliable. In fact, the early Indian expat workers were mostly unskilled people who were held in low regard by the local community.

In 1978, the young Ravi Pillai travelled to Saudi Arabia to lay the foundation for his business empire, fighting against the odds and trying to improve the status of expatriate Indian workers. Two years later, he established NSH CORPORATION (NSH), with 150 employees, and managed to handle more than a dozen contracts at a time, previously unheard of for an Indian in the region.

Ravi Pillai receiving the Padma Shri Award from the then President of India Pratibha Patil

A MILLION MILESTONES

During the initial years itself, Ravi Pillai took up defense-related construction contracts, won contracts with the Royal Air Terminal in Riyadh, made major headway in the oil and gas and petrochemical industries in Saudi Arabia. By this time, the number of workers under him had risen to five thousand. He went on creating jobs for the expatriates, but also hired skilled labour locally in huge numbers, and provided the best results by combining the power of diversity. The group was also recently awarded by Saudi ARAMCO's In Kingdom Total Value Add (IKTVA) Program which recognizes the prioritization of domestic value creation, and integration of localized talent.

With Ravi Pillai's efforts, the company flourished, winning contracts in every industry around them - petrochemical, refinery, steel plants, power plants, building complexes and civil construction, oil & gas, and high-rise buildings. The out of the box ideas, solutions, and impeccable efficiency, safety, and quality offered by the company were a step above the rest. Saudi Aramco, SABIC, ADNOC, Qatar Gas, Ras Gas, Maaden, KNPC, BAPCO, ALBA, ExxonMobil, Shell, Qatar Petroleum—a seemingly endless list of the large corporations of the world started admiring RP Group. Several of them formally acknowledged their appreciation of Ravi Pillai, with awards of excellence. Saudi Aramco, Ras Gas Qatar, and Exxon Mobil presented the Best Contractor Awards, Samsung with their Quality Excellence Awards, and Maaden with their Global Quality Excellence Award.

As a people's person, Dr. Ravi Pillai attributes much of his continuous success to his human capital, which is over 100,000 strong, expected to grow to 150,000 soon. He has also won awards for his determined focus on employee and site safety from various international corporations that he has worked with.

Dr. Ravi Pillai and Geetha Ravi Pillai, with Ganesh Pillai (son) and Anjana Ganesh Pillai (daughter-in-law), and Dr. Arathi Ravi Pillai (daughter) and Dr. Adithya Vishnu (son-in-law).

THE MIDAS TOUCH

Dr. Ravi Pillai, being one of the most successful businessmen in recent times, noticed the potential of tourism in his home state, much before anybody else did. For non-residents, there was a shortage of quality infrastructure to enjoy the beauty of Kerala, during their short visits. Thus was born the seed of the idea that led to Raviz Hotels and Resorts, beginning with Raviz Kollam. Raviz Kollam, the first tourism project of the group, provided a window to the wholesome, spellbinding experience that is God's Own Country. Raviz is a slice of the best of Kerala. It showcases the serene backwaters and lakes, various cultural and art forms of Kerala, Ayurvedic medical care, and treats you to the great gourmet and local cuisine. Raviz Kovalam, Kadavu Resort in Calicut, and Raviz Calicut, are other gems from the world of RP Group, offering the best of Kerala to the world. The Raviz resorts are among the most favoured wedding destinations in Kerala. Outside India, Versailles by Raviz, The Raviz Centre Point Hotel Dubai, and the Crowne Plaza in Dubai Marina are making their mark in the commercial hub of the Middle East.

The RP Group has made its mark in the retail sector, with RP Mall Kollam, RP Mall Calicut, RP Mall Coimbatore, RP Mall Thiruvananthapuram, and Blue Diamond Mall Calicut. They have ushered in a new standard in the retail business world.

Dr. Ravi Pillai also acquired and improved Upasana Hospital, and then founded the Nursing College, in his hometown, to provide the best healthcare and medical education. RP Group provides technical and vocational training to youth. His eagerness to bring quality education to all led to the establishment of schools. The academic world has recognized the New Millennium School, Bahrain, as one of the best and most sought-out centres of education in the country that boasts of producing fine young people with great discipline and high calibre.

MAKING A GREAT DIFFERENCE

While climbing the ladder of success, Dr. Ravi Pillai never forgot his fellow human beings. The RP Group takes its corporate social responsibility (CSR) very seriously and keeps aside 30% of its profits to help people. Dr. Ravi Pillai launched the RP Foundation, a charity organisation committed to uplifting the less fortunate. The Foundation carries out a number of charity projects globally. It is quite notable that the Foundation accepts funds only from RP Group, and doesn't receive any monetary assistance from other sources.

Over the years, Dr. Ravi Pillai has maintained a focus on the rehabilitation of those who suffer from incurable diseases, and the physically and differently-abled. He is running poverty eradication schemes through his Foundation. He has also spearheaded the effort towards the rehabilitation/assistance/damage coverage of the victims of the 2004 Tsunami, Gujarat earthquake, and those who were injured in the firework explosion at the Puttingal Devi Temple in Kerala. He has donated houses to over 250 families, donated to the cause of over 250 HIV-affected children (held under the 'Keraleeyam' initiative of Global Kerala), and continuously extends assistance to expats who find themselves in legal or other trouble.

The RP Foundation held mass wedding ceremonies for 400 couples in the years 2010 and 2013 and held a massive charity drive, 'Karunyaravam 2015' where aid was distributed to more than 15,000 people, by the then Chief Minister of Kerala, Oommen Chandy. The President of India and many dignitaries around the world commended Dr. Ravi Pillai for his service to the community. Recently, the RP Foundation has lent money, hand and foot, to the Covid-19 pandemic relief effort.

A PROMISING NEW GENERATION

A personal milestone and a proud feather in the cap for Dr. Ravi Pillai himself is the new generation of talented and dedicated engineers and other professionals who have joined RP Group in various capacities - they are the children of the semi-skilled people he had recruited years ago. While the RP Group prospered, its prosperity was well reflected in the individual fortunes of its employees too.

Dr. Ravi Pillai's unwavering attention to bringing progress and prosperity to his people and the generations to follow, in every way possible, has given rise to a myriad of establishments that focus on the skill, health, talent, and professional development of the youth.

Heart, soul, brain, power, wealth, and grace behind the RP Group and RP Foundation, Dr. Ravi Pillai has taken so much on over the years. His contributions are in construction, medicine, education, tourism, real estate, and a very efficient charity organization – and he has more than excelled in each of these sectors, making it nearly impossible to believe that it all came down to one person and his drive to found world-class enterprises. His story is like folklore or a myth, and it will leave a lasting mark on humanity for decades to come.

DR. B. RAVI PILLAI

Dr. B. Ravi Pillai, the billionaire entrepreneur and business magnate who helms the Ravi Pillai Group (RP Group), was born into a well-respected agricultural family in Kollam, Kerala, to Balakrishnan Pillai and Sharadamma. His RP Group is present in construction, hotels, real estate, hospitals, retail, and IT sectors, across continents.

Routinely featured on the Forbes Rich Lists, Dr. Ravi Pillai was one of the Top 600 global billionaires on Forbes World's Billionaires List-2019. Forbes even featured him on its cover. An inspirational figure, he has received several honours both in India and abroad, including the Times Now NRI of the Year Award. The Government of India awarded him the Pravasi Bharatiya Samman in 2008 and the civilian honour of Padma Shri in 2010 for his outstanding contributions in the fields of business and charity. Quite well-known in the global corporate world for his business acumen, Dr. Pillai is also highly regarded as a philanthropist. Excelsior College, New York bestowed an honorary doctorate on Ravi Pillai, years after he ended his formal education.

Dr. Ravi Pillai's wife, Geetha, runs the New Millennium School in Bahrain. They have a son, Ganesh Pillai, married to Anjana, and a daughter, Dr. Arathi, married to Dr. Adithya Vishnu.

3

BYJU'S MAGIC

This is the era when education is transacted through technology, spinning out the 'Ed-Tech' platform for learning. Interestingly, the world's most valuable startup in this field, the Bengaluru-based BYJU'S, was founded by a Malayali. Not many people are familiar with 'Think & Learn Pvt. Ltd.' but 'BYJU'S Learning App' is sure to ring a bell. BYJU'S is the first startup from Asia to attract capital investment from Facebook founder Mark Zuckerberg.

The Founder and CEO of 'BYJU'S Learning App,' Byju Raveendran, studied at the Malayalam-medium Government School in Azhikode. He was a bright student who bagged medals at Maths Olympiads and science quizzes. After clearing the 12th standard, Byju secured a B.Tech degree from the Kannur Engineering College. He then worked as a service engineer for a multinational shipping company.

The vacation trip to meet friends in Bengaluru during a year changed the course of Byju's life. He found all of them preparing to crack the Common Admission Test or CAT to secure admission to the Indian Institute of Management (IIM)'s MBA course. He turned into an impromptu trainer, helping them prepare for the test. At their insistence, he too took the exam as well. When the results were announced, guess who finished as the 'CAT Topper'? But Byju was preoccupied with another thought – "considered one of the toughest entrance tests, how did I crack the CAT exam without undergoing any prior coaching?" Then it dawned on Byju: "making learning fun and so simple for others helped me top the exam." All his efforts soon focused on sharing the same methods with others.

Byju Raveendran and his brother Riju Raveendran with their father Raveendran

In 2007, with the support of his friends, Byju started taking weekend CAT classes at Bengaluru's Jyoti Nivas College. His students soon realised that he made the learning process simpler and faster using some specific methods. The number of students in his classes rose from 50 to more than 1000. His CAT coaching classes then extended to the major cities in the country. Soon, Byju started coaching classes for other common entrance tests too.

Harnessing the power of technology to introduce quality and simplified learning solutions for students across the country, Byju started Think and Learn Pvt. Ltd. in 2011. Four years of intense work gave shape to a mobile application to deliver mathematics and science content to school children. In August 2015, Byju launched BYJU'S - The Learning App, enabling children to study at home using the mobile application. It helped them learn effectively and independently — the app first made available the content for children from Class IV to XII. Within two years, it secured 80 lakh downloads. Today, students from more than 1700 cities, towns, and villages of India benefit from the app. BYJU'S App can be downloaded for free from Google Play Store and Apple iOS app store. Those who want to access more content can do so by paying a fee. As per November 2021 data, over 100 million students used the app.

Outstanding teachers are on board to develop lessons in-house for the app. Videos and graphics too are created to present the content. The learning app offers ways to assess each student's progress, resolve any shortcomings, and improve learning. Byju Raveendran says the app has been designed to make learning easy and fun-filled. He is sure that once children begin to enjoy the learning process, they will study without any prompting from their parents.

More than 90 percent of parents who took part in a survey said that their children had shown considerable improvement in learning after using BYJU'S App. This brought Mark Zuckerberg, founder of Facebook, to invest in BYJU'S. With his wife, Dr. Priscilla Chan, Zuckerberg invested in BYJU'S App through the Chan-Zuckerberg Initiative in their first such entry in Asia. In his Facebook post, Mark Zuckerberg stated that Byju's conceived and delivered the learning process easily and effectively, suiting the needs of a child. Zuckerberg also mentioned that the partnership with

BYJU'S aimed to make this latest mode of learning available to more students worldwide.

Furthermore, BYJU'S, in association with Walt Disney, also developed a 'Disney. BYJU'S Early Learn' app for children of Class I to III. This app deploys popular Disney characters to impart lessons to the little ones through stories, games, and videos.

The company continues to grow with acquisitions as well. These deals include an approx. $1 billion buy of New Delhi-based Aakash Educational Services Limited (AESL) and the $600 million purchase of Singapore-headquartered Great Learning, a leading global player in professional and higher education, in 2021. In August 2020, BYJU'S acquired Mumbai-based coding start-up WhiteHat Jr for $300 million. Before it, in 2019, the company had acquired US-based Osmo, a company that designs Augmented Reality (AR) games for children, for $120 million.

Today, BYJU'S remains the Ed-Tech startup to receive the highest capital investment in the world. According to business information providing platform Crunchbase, from 2013 to 2021, BYJU'S has attracted $3.2 Billion as capital investment. With capital investment coming in from various companies and investors, the company's net value increased to $18 billion in 2021, that's about Rs.1,35,000 crore. Byju, who has a 34 percent share in the firm along with his family members, made it to the Forbes Rich List 2019. According to Forbes India Rich List 2021, Byju Raveendran and his family were on the 47th rank, with a net worth of $4.05B.

From bringing Bollywood superstar Shahrukh Khan as the brand ambassador to earning the pride of place on the official jersey of the Indian Cricket team, BYJU'S has become a household name with prudent marketing forays.

Byju Raveendran with his wife and co-founder Divya Gokulnath

Byju says he will continue his research for avant-garde learning processes to ensure greater individual benefit. He also focuses on devising new methods that align with the company's successfully tested formula - to keep learning simple, fun-filled, and effective. Having gained enormous public trust in a short span, BYJU'S now aims to empower more children worldwide.

"I am an engineer by profession, teacher by passion, and an accidental entrepreneur. I did not come into this field because I wanted to become an entrepreneur. Teaching was my driving force when I realised that I could make learning easy for others. As I wanted to share my learning ideology with every student around the world, that's when I thought of starting BYJU'S. I am fortunate that my passion and profession align with each other and I get to do what I love," says Byju Raveendran. He advises new entrepreneurs to take risks, never be afraid of failure, and develop ventures around their passion that can bring about a change in society.

BYJU RAVEENDRAN

Byju Raveendran, the Founder and CEO of 'Think & Learn Pvt. Ltd.,' the parent company of BYJU'S Learning App, is the youngest Malayali to find a place on the Forbes Rich List. According to Forbes, as of 2021, Byju, his wife Divya Gokulnath, and his brother Riju Raveendran have a combined net worth of $4.05 billion.

Byju was born in Azhikode, a small village in the district of Kannur in Kerala, to Raveendran and Shobhanavalli, both teachers. Byju was a self-learner from a young age and developed different learning methods to understand and deliver concepts better. Mark Zuckerberg, Tencent, Sequoia Capital, Naspers, General Atlantic, and other global giants have invested in BYJU'S.

Byju's wife, Divya Gokulnath, is the co-founder of BYJU'S. The couple has two sons, Nish and Nivin.

4

WHERE DREAMS LEAD...

Senapathy, running a small-scale plumbing materials store in Thiruvananthapuram, aspired his son to be a medical doctor. The Senapathy family did not have a doctor member, while young Gopalakrishnan wasn't bad in his studies. These factors prompted Senapathy to think on those lines.

After completing his Pre-Degree Course, Gopalakrishnan applied for MBBS at Thiruvananthapuram Medical College (there was no medical entrance exam at that time). He missed the seat for just two marks, but the 17-year-old was not going to waste his time moping around.

He enrolled at the Thiruvananthapuram University College for a bachelor's degree course in Physics. In three years, he graduated with flying colours and joined IIT Madras for a post-graduation course. Little did he know then that the IIT would play a transformative role in his life. One day in 1977, the 22-year-old Gopalakrishnan was pedalling back to the hostel after spending time at the vast library on the IIT campus. He had fitted numerous books on Computer Science, borrowed from the library, on the carrier of the cycle.

Professor H.N.Mahabala, who was passing by, noticed young Gopalakrishnan moving through the track with the pile of books and called out to him. The professor informed him of an upcoming seminar on the myriad Computer Science possibilities. "It will do you good if you attend it," he said. Gopalakrishnan promptly followed his advice. S. Gopalakrishnan, a.k.a Kris Gopalakrishnan, can now recall the seminar as the distinct moment that made him realise that computer science would be his path forward.

His newfound passion prompted him to enroll for an MTech at the same institute in Computer Science. Soon after passing the course, he joined Patni Computer Solutions, an IT company, in 1979, where his friends 'rechristened' him Kris. One more defining moment in his life came later when he met another Computer Science engineer N.R. Narayana Murthy.

In 1980, Narayana Murthy let Kris in on his plan to start a new venture. At just 25, Kris was ready to take the plunge, confident that he could always look for another job in case the new enterprise failed. His family was not opposed to the idea either. Amidst all these, his marriage was arranged.

Kris Gopalakrishnan with N.R.Narayana Murthy, co- founder of Infosys

After the marriage ceremony, Kris dropped the bombshell! He told his wife Sudha that he intended to resign from his job to start a new company. But she was cool as a cucumber! She just approved of his move. The rest is history; Infosys was launched at the end of 1981. Apart from Murthy, Kris, and K. Dinesh, the 'gang' of co-founders had Ashok Arora, Nandan Nilekani, N.S.Raghavan and another Malayali S.D. Shibulal, all engineers from Patni.

The first project was from the USA, with which Infosys began to take its baby steps. Many a time, there was a dire need of funds, and this was before Venture Capital Funds became so popular. Kris recalls that the team had to face tough challenges during their entrepreneurial journey. Foremost amongst them was the collapse of a joint venture with an American company K.S.A. in 1989.

This time a company came forward, offering to take over Infosys. But Narayana Murthy and Kris Gopalakrishnan were not ready to let go of the company they had built from scratch. One of the co-founders, Ashok Arora, chose to press the exit button. Kris recalls the phase as one of the most testing ones in his entrepreneurial life.

Soon, through sheer resilience, Infosys and Infoscions forged ahead. Shares were made available on the capital market through Initial Public Offering (IPO). But no one was willing to buy the entire lot. Finally, the IPO was fully subscribed, with American investment bank Morgan Stanley taking 13 percent of the total number of shares on offer. Another side of history is that Infosys shares later became one of India's most sought after, with the company becoming an IT bellwether.

The lessons Kris Senapathy Gopalakrishnan has learned in his three-and-a-half decades as an entrepreneur are many – the relevance of honesty and values is chief among them. Kris likens business to a marathon. "Business is not a 100m race," he says. "Honesty counts if one is to complete a business marathon successfully. It will win support from all fronts, employees, business partners, the government, and society. It is important to brainstorm for new ideas to make strides in business. Progress will be possible only through change. So, learning should be a constant process," he elaborates. Infosys sets aside four percent of its total profit for training programmes and educational purposes.

Kris Gopalakrishnan (second from left) along with Infosys co-founders
Nandan Nilekani, N.R.Narayana Murthy, N.S.Raghavan, K.Dinesh, and S.D.Shibulal

After stepping down as the Vice Chairman of Infosys, he is actively shaping the technology and startup ecosystem through a myriad of roles. Kris is the chairman of Axilor Ventures, an early stage startup accelerator and venture fund. He is also the chairman of itihaasa Research and Digital, a not-for-profit think-tank focused on the evolution of technology domains in India. The Reserve Bank of India (RBI) has appointed Kris Gopalakrishnan as the first Chairperson of the Reserve Bank Innovation

Hub (RBIH) in 2020. He serves on the Board of Governors of Okinawa Institute of Science and Technology (OIST) and is the chairman, Board of Governors of IIIT, Bangalore.

He once said, startups in India need to become household names and they should create Internet successes on the lines of Facebook and Google. "We need our own Facebook and Google".

Sharing his thoughts, Kris says, "Any work should be carried out with utmost perfection. Approach everything with respect; only then will it be reciprocated. It is possible to win the respect of employees by creating a quality work environment and making shares available through Employee Stock Options (ESOP). Similarly, paying tax on time will gain the respect of the government. The work should conform to global standards. You can't predict from where competition comes. Indian companies should be made competitive at the international level."

He adds that ideas are important on the entrepreneurial path, and great ventures are born from innovative ideas. But Kris Gopalakrishnan also believes that the real winners are those who remain humble even when they are at the top of their game.

SENAPATHY 'KRIS' GOPALAKRISHNAN

Kris Gopalakrishnan is a co-founder of Infosys, one of the largest IT companies in India. He became the Managing Director and CEO of the company in 2007. Within four years of Kris at the helm, the company's income doubled to $ 6 billion. In August 2011, he was anointed Executive Vice-Chairman. Three years later, in October 2014, Kris hung up his boots. The Hurun India Rich List values Kris Gopalakrishnan at Rs 35,200 Crore and with a donation of Rs.50 Crore, he has been ranked by Hurun as the 19th most generous Indian in 2021 Hurun India Philanthorpy List.

In 2014, he founded Axilor Ventures to provide a helping hand to start-ups with venture capital funds and other necessary support. Kris also launched 'Itihaasa,' a digital app documenting the history of IT in India. Kris became president of the Confederation of Indian Industry (CII) during 2013-14. In 2011, the nation honoured him with the Padma Bhushan. He resides in Bangalore with his family. Kris is married to Sudha, and they have a daughter Meghana.

5

THE EMPEROR OF 'PURE' GOLD

The early beginning of T.S.Kalyanaraman's success story reminds us of a monochrome flashback set in a quaint, sleepy old-world Thrissur in the late 1950s. Kalyanaraman was the eldest son of T.K. Seetharam Iyer, a textile businessman in Thrissur.

Kalyanaraman learned his trade by working behind the counter at the textile shop run by his father. While still a student at Thrissur Model Boys High School, he would help his father at the shop during school holidays and vacations. Under the guidance of Seetharam Iyer, Kalyanaraman picked up the fine art of understanding customer psyche and learnt to understand their needs and interests.

After finishing his B.Com from Kerala Varma College in Thrissur, he dived entirely into his father's textile business to help increase its presence in the state. So much so that Kalyanaraman successfully transformed Kalyan in Thrissur into a fashion destination for wedding purchases.

The father-son duo did not compromise on the quality of the products sold at their outlets, and soon the approach propelled Kalyan to new heights. In fact, it was the customers' feedback that encouraged Kalyanaraman to enter the gold business, later in 1993. Many of his customers said they would confidently purchase gold from Kalyanaraman if he started a jewellery outlet.

T.S.Kalyanaraman, Rajesh Kalyanaraman, Ramesh Kalyanaraman and Karthik Ramani with Prime Minister Narendra Modi

He set out to do the required groundwork, first visiting shops in Kerala and neighbouring Tamil Nadu. In the beginning of the 90s, most jewellery shops were not larger than 400 square feet in area. The ready stock was limited and jewellers custom-made ornaments as per the requirement and designs provided by clients. However, Kalyanaraman was determined to revolutionise their showroom and customer experience. With his expertise in managing textile showrooms, it was not difficult for Kalyanaraman to gauge the purchasing psychology of Malayali customers. He understood they were ever happier to see better alternatives. He decided to emulate the spacious settings of textile showrooms while designing his new gold showroom. The jewellery showroom offered customers plenty of options in gold designs and styles.

He had Seetharam Iyer's consent for the venture. Kalyanaraman entered the gold business in 1993, with an initial capital of Rs. 75 lakhs. Near the renowned Paramekkavu Temple in Thrissur, he set up Kalyan Jewellers — a gold ornaments showroom spread across a sprawling 4,000 square feet setup, a first of its kind in Kerala's perennially buzzing gold market.

Funny though, there was plenty of lip service when Kalyan Jewellers opened its first showroom at Paramekkavu. Many advised Kalyanaraman to be cautious, considering the huge maintenance required for a gold showroom. However, he never let unwarranted scepticism overshadow his determination. In fact, the newly opened jewellery showroom witnessed a massive influx of customers. Kalyan Jewellers offered customers a new gold shopping experience. It marked the beginning of a golden era for the retail jewellery market in the state.

Kalyanaraman ensured that the progress of his business was at a healthy pace. His elder son Rajesh joined the business after finishing his higher studies. Ramesh, Kalyanaraman's younger son, too joined shortly. Soon, he was mulling over the launch of new additional showrooms, the idea being devoting one showroom each to his children.

The gold maverick picked Palakkad to launch his new branch. It was the perfect choice as people of the district mostly travelled to Thrissur or Coimbatore for large purchases, especially gold, since Palakkad didn't have many jewellery shops. Soon the Palakkad showroom turned into a huge hit.

Kalyanaraman set new trends that brought transparency to the gold market. The 'price tag' on jewellery items displayed the wages for making an ornament, which was a surprising introduction to the market. Kalyan

Jewellers was the pioneer in implementing 'hallmarking,' a symbol of the purity of gold. Another novel idea was to have a chain of customer awareness centres named 'My Kalyan' to make customers aware of an ornament's purity, hallmarking and making charges. These later turned into mini stores. Without much delay, Kalyan Jewellers forayed into selling diamonds as well.

T.S.Kalyanaraman with his sons Rajesh Kalyanaraman and Ramesh Kalyanaraman

The scaling up happened gradually. Kalyanaraman paid due diligence to pick locations for new branches. Kalyan Jewellers opened new showrooms in Coimbatore in 2003, Bengaluru in 2008, and Andhra Pradesh later in the same year. After commanding a dominant market share in South India, the jewellery major moved to the Western part of the country, opening a branch in Ahmedabad (Gujarat is the largest hub of diamond business in India). Each debut – be it Palakkad, Coimbatore, Bengaluru, or Ahmedabad — resulted from the expert's precise market research. He takes a keen interest in arranging ornaments according to the taste and interests of the customers of each new market. He took goldsmiths onboard from different parts of the country, each of them skilled in design, developing regional trends, and making region-specific traditional ornaments. Apart from this, Kalyan Jewellers developed its own unique designs too.

AMBASSADORS OF PURE GOLD

Actors like Mammootty and Amitabh Bachchan have partnered with Kalyan as brand ambassadors, scripting a rich legacy for the brand. The Bachchan family, comprising Amitabh Bachchan, Jaya Bachchan and Aishwarya Rai Bachchan, too joined Kalyan as brand ambassadors. In every state, celebrities with a niche were made brand ambassadors. Today, Kalyan has a glittering line up of celebrities as brand ambassadors.

Kalyan's rapid growth prompted Kalyanaraman to ratchet up his work and lifestyle to the next level. For a high-profile businessman, time translates into money so naturally. So, he bought his first private jet, 'Embraer Phenom,' in 2012. He also owns a helicopter, enabling him to reach those showrooms that do not have an airstrip nearby. Ever since his trade horizons expanded beyond the country's borders, he acquired the 'Embraer Legacy 650', an aircraft that can fly for eight-and-a-half hours non-stop.

Brand Kalyan forayed to the international market by launching six new showrooms in the UAE. In 2013, the total number of showrooms crossed 50.

In 2014, Kalyan Jewellers received a capital investment of Rs. 1,200 Crore from the global private equity firm Warburg Pincus. This was the biggest foreign investment ever made in the Indian retail jewellery market. The FPI gave a fillip to the capital expansion activities of Kalyan Jewellers. The inauguration of three showrooms in Kolkata in 2016 took Kalyan to the milestone of 100 showrooms. By August 2018, Kalyan Jewellers could set up 100 showrooms in India alone, and now the Company has achieved the milestone of 150 showrooms, globally. At present, Kalyan Jewellers employs more than 8,000 people.

Kalyanaraman says the brand will continue to expand to more countries. Against the backdrop of a rise in online jewellery shopping, they took over 'Candere,' an online jewellery marketing company in 2017, and established their presence in the digital field. Apart from the jewellery business, Kalyan has set out to the real estate, under the banner Kalyan Developers, constructing residential complexes in major cities of Kerala. The annual turnover of the group is around Rs 10,000 Crore.

PAYING IT BACK

Kalyanaraman makes it a priority to keep aside a share of profits for social welfare activities. He has developed a scheme to build 2,000 homes for the chosen underprivileged across the country. This initiative is implemented in association with a non-profit organization 'Habitat for Humanity India.'

'The value of trust' is the biggest factor Kalyanaraman has identified during his years of entrepreneurship. So, the brand's now-famous slogan 'Trust, isn't it everything?' as reminded by all their brand ambassadors at the end of their advertisements, is more than just a tagline. He is also confident about the unflinching trust customers have in the gold they buy from Kalyan. He is sure that his customer base of 20 lakh people mostly is repeat customers.

"Never yearn for profit. It comes on its own. If quality products are sold at reasonable prices, sales will increase. As sales increase, so does profit," Kalyanaraman recalls the lessons passed on by his father. He passes them down to the next generation too. Kalyanaraman asserts that business is nothing but pleasure. He does not take it as a burden or a strain on him. He prioritizes spending his leisure time with family members. "We go together to watch movies. We go for vacations also together every year," he says.

T.S. KALYANARAMAN

T.S. Kalyanaraman is the Chairman and Managing Director of Kalyan Jewellers, one of India's largest retail jewellery groups with a growing presence in the Middle East. He was born in 1947 to T.K. Seetharam Iyer and Narayaniyammal. He has been on the Forbes Billionaires List since 2013. According to the Forbes Billionaires list of 2018, he owns assets worth Rs 10,000 crore. He is the president of the Kerala Jewellers Federation (KJF), a collective of prominent jewellery groups in Kerala.

Kalyanaraman is married to Ramadevi. His children are Rajesh Kalyanaraman (Executive Director handling finance and purchase of Kalyan Jewellers), Ramesh Kalyanaraman (Executive Director overseeing marketing and operations, Kalyan Jewellers), and Radhika. The son-and-daughters-in-law are Karthik Ramani (Managing Director, Kalyan Developers), Maya Rajesh and Deepa Ramesh.

6

LABOUR OF LOVE

P.N.C. Menon faced many hardships early on. He lost his father when he was just 10. The incident shook his family and the very foundations of his childhood. Fate had more hurdles in store to throw in his way. His mother turned ill, and he spent a significant part of his early years looking after his mom while children of his age indulged in the simpler joys of childhood. Such circumstances in his life early shaped him to take on responsibilities without hesitation.

In 1976 fortune finally smiled upon him when he met an Omani gentleman named Sulaiman Al Adawi at a hotel lobby in Kochi. By that time, young P.N.C. Menon had already begun his journey in business with small-scale interior design projects and furniture business in Kochi and Bengaluru. Al Adawi had come to the port city to purchase a fishing boat. He invited Menon to Oman, telling him about the vast business opportunities that the desert country held.

Dreams of expanding his business and buying oil wells kept his curious and zealous mind occupied. Finally, after almost three months of his encounter with Sulaiman, Menon received a visa from Oman. With a Rs.50 note in his pocket, he left for the Arab country. Little did Menon know then that he had embarked on a journey that would change his life forever. He was led to a new path where he would become P.N.C Menon, the real estate entrepreneur who would leave his mark on many high-rise buildings and palaces in India and the Gulf.

Young Menon was under the notion that in Oman, all wealthy owned oil wells where they produced petroleum and sold it for a huge profit. He assumed that Sulaiman, who had brought him to Oman, also owned several oil wells. But once he got there, it was time for a reality check. Sulaiman wasn't rich but a middle-class man who was a captain with the Royal Army of Oman. Slightly fazed by his naivety but completely undaunted, Menon remained optimistic.

Meanwhile, days turned into weeks without any opportunity in sight. By the end of that month, Menon turned utterly restless. He asked Sulaiman, "What is our plan?" Sulaiman spoke reassuringly, "Don't worry. How much will it cost to start a business?" Menon took stock of the situation and calculated that he would need at least OMR3000. Sulaiman, like a dutiful friend, immediately arranged for a loan from a bank. Just like he did back home, Menon started the business by taking up interior design projects. The venture was named 'Services and Trade Company' (S.T.C.). Work stretched to more than 12 hours a day, and slowly but surely, the business began to take off.

P.N.C.Menon receiving Pravasi Bharatiya Samman
from the then President of India Pratibha Patil

Soon after, Menon realized that only big contracts would allow the company to grow and started putting more effort into catching bigger fish. In 1984, he won the contract to design the interiors of the Sultan of Oman's offices. It set P.N.C. Menon's entrepreneurial life in gear. Menon, who believes that striving for a high work standard is ingrained in his DNA, was able to leave an impression with the quality of his projects. Coveted contracts of palaces of the royal families of Oman, Qatar, Bahrain, and Brunei sought him out soon. By the end of the '80s, he forayed into the construction industry. The company offered planning, construction, and interior design services and could do roaring business. In the early '90s, he branched out to Dubai with a construction company.

HOMECOMING

Menon, who is firmly rooted in his soil, wished to start an establishment in India. He was eager to explore the untapped potential of the Indian market. It led to the inception of 'Sobha Developers.' In 1995, after much strategizing, he picked Bengaluru as the company's headquarters. He was keen on turning Sobha Developers into a national player in the real estate sector. Sobha arrived on the scene when real estate was perceived to be a sector with regional limitations. Armed with years of international exposure, Menon laid all such notions to rest.

Today Sobha's residential complexes span Bengaluru, Kochi, Kozhikode, Thrissur, Coimbatore, Mysuru, Chennai, Pune, and Delhi straddling hundreds of projects finished on a contract basis, including five-star hotels and headquarters for corporate companies. Sobha has erected building complexes for Infosys, HCL, Dell, Bosch, Biocon, Taj Hotels, and ITC Hotels. The Sobha Group has done more than 80 percent of Infosys' construction activities. Over two decades, it grew into India's best real estate brand. In 2006, the company's shares were listed on the stock exchange through Initial Public Offering (IPO). The number of applications received was 126 times higher than the number of shares put up for sales. Sobha Developers, which started its journey from India with Rs.30 crore, became a company with over Rs.5000 crore market value.

During this time, the sweeping changes in the Gulf prompted the company to relocate its headquarters from Oman to Dubai. Sobha Group has construction projects to the tune of Rs. 2 lakh crore in Dubai. Mohammed bin Rashid Al Maktoum City, also known as District One, is Menon's dream project, coming up in the heart of Dubai, in association with the Meydan Group. Sobha International also has plans to expand to other regions, including Europe.

Even after becoming one of the most successful entrepreneurs today, P.N.C. Menon likes to keep experimenting with new prospects. When asked if he expected to taste the success of this scale while running an interior design business in India, he said, "No one really plans to become a millionaire. It is purely coincidental. When we stand at the first step of entrepreneurship, the next thought is only about the fifth and then the tenth step. There's no thought about the hundredth step at the starting line. When we're climbing the tenth step, we may only think as far as the twenty-fifth step. That is how people reach the top, one step at a time." He feels that no entrepreneur should set out to chase money and adds that one should chase only success while wealth comes as a by-product.

But such laudatory feats would not have been possible without the four cornerstones of his life - his wife Sobha, after whom his company is named, and his children Bindu, Ravi, and Revathi. Currently, eldest daughter Bindu is the Director of Sobha Group in Dubai, and son Ravi serves as the Chairman of Sobha Limited in India. The youngest daughter Revathi is settled in Dubai with her family.

P.N.C. Menon believes that success becomes possible only when one moves forward with dedication while steadfastly being credible. He believes in keeping a portion of one's wealth to help society. He has set aside half of his earnings for charitable activities. They are carried out under Sri Kurumba Educational and Charitable Trust. This trust has initiated several philanthropic activities in six villages under Vadakkenchery, Kizhakkanchery and Kannambra panchayats of Palakkad district since 2006 under the 'Gramasobha' scheme.

P.N.C.Menon, wife Sobha and family

Along with Sobha Hermitage for senior citizens and widows and a primary health centre (PHC), the Gramasobha scheme raised the standards of students in government schools through Sobha Icon. It also conducts dowry-free community marriages for girls and arranges marital counselling to secure their family life. The Sobha Academy and Sobha Icon ensures high-quality education for poor children where food is also provided free of cost. The beneficiaries of the social welfare programmes are treated with utmost dignity. When Menon visits his hometown, he tries to find time to enquire about their well-being. The Sri Kurumba Trust intends to extend its initiatives in due course to other parts of India, starting with Karnataka, for which, preparations are already underway.

It is amazing to find how a young boy who faced so many misfortunes so early on in life dared to tackle his future with great gusto. Any ordinary human being would probably have given it all up to the workings of destiny. But Menon, a diamond in the rough, let the calamities in his life shape him to outshine everyone, leaving people in awe of his prowess.

P.N.C. MENON

A diamond's origins lie amongst stones. It doesn't start out polished but is turned into a precious gem under immense pressure. Human nature is somewhat similar. It is only by going through perilous situations that one emerges a reformed person. Such people overcome their shortcomings and cross every obstacle by learning from their failures. Those born with a silver spoon in their mouth seldom have the same ardour to reach the pinnacle of success. Puthan Naduvakkatt Chenthamaraksha Menon, better known as P.N.C. Menon, is one such celebrated entrepreneur whose zest for growth is exemplary.

The founder of Sobha Group, P.N.C. Menon, has his businesses spread across India and countries in the Gulf region. He owns industrial enterprises spanning real estate, contract construction, interior design, and furniture production. His accomplishments are approved by many an august circle of leaders and businessmen. No wonder, he was bestowed Oman citizenship in 1997 for his business achievements in that country.

Hurun India Rich List 2021 valued his assets at $1.82 billion (Rs.13,700 crore). He has received numerous awards, including the Institute of Directors (IOD) 'Golden Peacock Lifetime Achievement Award.' In 2009, he was honoured with the Pravasi Bhartiya Samman.

7

BUSINESSMAN
WITH A HEART OF GOLD

A long time ago, across the Arabian Sea, there was a land with golden sand and several ancient mysteries. We now call that land the Emirates. From the final decades of the last millennium, Malayalis called this land their home away from home. Enter any Gulf nation, and you are sure to find a Malayali. One such Malayali took the entrepreneurial route and established himself there in 1987 in the gold and diamond jewellery business. It is Joy Alukkas, the businessman with a heart of gold.

Born as the fourth son of renowned jeweller Varghese Alukkas, Joy grew up with a passion to be an entrepreneur. When Joy was born in 1956, his father set up a small gold & jewellery retail store in Thrissur. While studying, Joy learned the ropes of the business from his father as well and was ready to spread his wings at a very young age. During the late 80s, the Gulf was the rage in every Malayali household. Joy's interest in the Middle East picked up once customers from the Gulf started coming to his father's store for their wedding jewellery purchases.

Joy was eager to see what awaited him in the land of black gold and flew to Dubai in 1986. He visited many gold shops and understood the nature of trade there. While most of the goldsmiths were Gujaratis, the Malayalis took the lead in sales and marketing. The best part? Most of the customers were from God's Own Country, Kerala, as it was a fad for them to buy gold from the Gulf countries. It did not take long for young Joy to put two and two together to realize that there was a goldmine for him there to explore. He thought if Malayalis were the big customers in the Gulf, it absolutely made sense for a businessman from Kerala to commence operations to serve the Malayalis.

Joy Alukkas receiving Dubai Quality Awards Certification from Sheikh Mohammed Bin Rashid Al Maktoum, Vice President and Prime Minister of the UAE. His son John Paul Alukkas is nearby.

Upon his return, he spoke to his father about opening a showroom in the UAE. However, he did not immediately get a nod from his family as the Iran-Iraq war was at its peak. They were worried about his safety. But Joy did not give up and patiently explained to his father about the potential of the jewellery business in the Gulf. Eventually, his father gave in, and Joy Alukkas opened his first jewellery showroom in Abu Dhabi in 1987.

Half a year later, he opened his second showroom in Dubai. However, like many other businesses he also had to shut shop in 1990 due to the Gulf war but resumed his business immediately after the war in the year 1991.

Apart from making pure gold available, he was a pioneer in launching many unique campaigns, including grand prize schemes to excite people to purchase gold & diamond jewellery. Joy expanded his jewellery chain in the UAE on his own, but it was still run as a part of the family business, i.e., Alukkas International.

He kept expanding his showrooms in the Gulf and soon took over the operations as his own in the coming years. In 2002, Joy opened his first showroom in India at Kottayam, Kerala. Later, he returned to Dubai with plans to create a global brand under his own name. He renamed his business as 'Joyalukkas.'

Joy had set his goal to expand his empire across ten countries and establish over 100 showrooms by 2010. Joyalukkas Jewellery, today, is a 140 showroom retail chain spread across 11 countries –85 showrooms in India and the rest across the Middle East, USA, United Kingdom, Singapore and Malaysia. The group's India headquarters is in Thrissur, Kerala and the headquarters for the international operations is in Dubai, UAE.

Joy Alukkas believes that one can achieve great things by setting a goal. "If we had not set big goals, we would not be where we are today," he says as he sits in his home 'Joy Alukkas Mansion' in Thrissur Sobha City.

From the start, Joy focused on bringing professionalism and having a network of showrooms. Hence, he could surpass the other jewellery chains. He encouraged the consumers to insist on bills to bring a culture of transparency and trust.

Joy Alukkas has always been at the forefront of providing quality gold in unique designs while setting new trends. Valuable offers, facilities and prompt customer services were also ensured. Joyalukkas became the first retail jewellery chain to achieve ISO 9001, ISO 14001 certifications and entered the LIMCA Book of World Records by opening the world's largest jewellery showroom in Chennai.

Joy Alukkas and wife Jolly Joy with family

Joy Alukkas did not have a walkover in India. Having showrooms in towns without a jewellery-buying culture, thefts and fires came in his way of smooth business handling. But the resolute entrepreneur battled everything with a clear goal and vision.

The Joyalukkas Group business is not limited to jewellery. The other group operations include Shopping Mall branded Mall of Joy, currently in Kottayam; Fashion & textiles branded Jolly Silks; a strong Money Exchange arm based in UAE, Kuwait & Oman under the brand name 'Joyalukkas Money Exchange.' He also made his presence felt in realty through 'Joyalukkas Lifestyle Developers' with one project, Joyalukkas Gold Tower, Kochi.

The group has about 8,000 employees in various ventures. Joy says being able to help create a living for so many people is the most satisfying element in his life. When creating wealth, Joy ensures that he spends a good portion on charity. Charitable activities are managed under the CSR wing which is called, the Joyalukkas Foundation.

JOYALUKKAS FOUNDATION

Joyalukkas Foundation consistently undertakes various programs to help the needy and encourages causes that benefit society. From building homes to helping flood victims, blood donations or conducting health camps, Joy and his wife Jolly believe in being there when needed the most. Under Joyalukkas Foundation, he has built old-age homes, initiated measures to build houses and provide medical assistance to the poor. Currently, in Kerala, 250 houses have been committed to people who have lost their homes during the 2018 floods, under the initiative 'Joy Homes.' Many of the committed homes have already been built and handed over. Joy aspires to do charity work in the same spirit as he does business, with 100% passion and commitment.

JOY'S ADVICE TO BUDDING ENTREPRENEURS

Being an entrepreneur, he has learned numerous lessons. He says one should not hesitate to absorb the good attributes of people around him. Many businesses fail because of the lack of humility to listen and learn new things from around.

Joy Alukkas advises entrepreneurs to start the entrepreneurial journey only after working with someone for two-three years. "Making quick decisions and getting things done in the right way are essential for succeeding in business. Good opportunities will be lost if we sit contemplating," he says.

JOY ALUKKAS

Joy Alukkas is the Chairman and Managing Director of Joyalukkas Group, a multi-billion dollar organisation spread across India, USA, UK, Singapore, Malaysia & GCC countries. He has earned the reputation of being the 'Man with the Midas Touch' for his many successful endeavours in the world of business.

Joy Alukkas has won numerous national and international awards including NDTV, Superbrands, the Times Group, Retail Middle East, Arabian Business Magazine and the Gem and Jewellery Trade Council Awards. He has also figured in the Forbes and the Hurun lists. The Hurun India Rich List 2021 valued his wealth at Rs.18,200 crore.

His wife Jolly Joy spearheads Joyalukkas Foundation, the Corporate Social Responsibility division of the group. He has 3 children, son, John Paul is the Managing Director of Joyalukkas International Operations and is married to Sonia. His daughter Mary Antony is married to Antony Jos, Managing Director, Joyalukkas Exchange. His youngest daughter Elsa is married to Thomas, an engineer in the US.

8

NEVER SAY DIE

The unassuming locality in Thrissur and the middle class household where Kochouseph grew up did not give indications that they were nurturing a prodigy. He grew up like any middle-class family's child. Interestingly, he was weak in Mathematics, writing 6 instead of 9 or vice-versa, his additions and subtractions invariably going wrong. However, Physics became his strength later on, so it was only natural for him to complete his graduation and post-graduation in Physics from Saint Thomas College, Thrissur.

He wanted to become an ISRO scientist during his college days. But two to three months after his post-graduation, Kochouseph was yet to land a job. Finally, he joined a small electronics company in Thiruvananthapuram as a supervisor trainee with a stipend of Rs.150. The company manufactured emergency lamps, battery chargers, stabilizers, and the like. A year later, he moved to another company in the same city. His dream of becoming a scientist may not have been fulfilled, but his ardour hadn't diminished in the least. The company recognised his calibre and, considering his outstanding performance, assigned him more responsibilities. Within a short period, he became the technical as well as research head of the firm.

Soon he became an expert at repairing electronic devices. Many people approached him to repair electrical appliances, mainly stabilizers. This encouraged him to nurture a new aspiration, one that was going to revolutionise the appliance industry as we know it now. He thought about starting his own venture for manufacturing stabilizers with the knowledge he had accumulated so far. With the asset of his work experience and almost zero capital in his bank account, he left his job and confided in his father. Always supportive of his son's aspirations, Kochouseph's father gave him Rs.50,000.

Kochouseph Chittilappilly with his wife Sheela Kochouseph

BUILDING AN EMPIRE

All he had to do was choose a place to start. After much deliberation, he concluded that his hometown would not be an ideal place. If he were to fail, the last thing he wanted was the sympathy or ridicule of friends and extended family. So, he set forth to Kochi. At two hours from Thrissur, it wasn't too far from home. He rented a shed to start work. Since stabilizers are used to protect home appliances from voltage variations, he named his product 'V-Guard.' He also designed the logo. That is how, in 1977, his first stabilizer was made with production starting commercially at the manufacturing unit in Kaloor.

With four to five stabilizers in hand, Kochouseph felt confident enough to venture out in search of customers. He visited many shops, but a positive response was not forthcoming. Then, the use of stabilizers was limited to refrigerators, an appliance found in wealthy houses. Popular giants like Keltron and Tata were already ruling the market. V-Guard was priced comparatively higher than its competitors. Keltron's stabilizer was only Rs. 490 whereas V-Guard was Rs. 495. The shop owners were hesitant to buy his product. But Kochouseph, aware of the shortcomings in other stabilizers, confidently focused on addressing all those issues in his product and sold refined pieces. He offered the shopkeepers a higher margin, assuring them that he would take back the product in case of any complaints. Much to their relief, he told them to pay him only after the product was sold. When the shopkeepers found that they hadn't received any complaints from customers, they came to trust his products, and the business began to boom. Kochouseph was determined not to compromise on the quality of his product. His honest approach worked, resulting in V-Guard's success. Soon afterward, Kochouseph needed more capital to support his growing enterprise. When the banks rejected his loan applications, his father, forever his pillar of strength, gave him another Rs 50,000.

A year after beginning his venture, giving into his father's desire that he get married, Kochouseph married Sheela. She later launched her enterprise, V-Star Creations, a clothing brand. With the family's support, V-Guard stabilizers slowly started conquering the Kerala market. During the early 90s, when many young Indians sought their fortunes in the Middle East, it began to reflect in the form of better lifestyles for their families back home. The result? Numerous electronic products were introduced to Kerala homes. The electricity supply was not stable enough to support the new influx of products. Kochouseph, being a true entrepreneur, took advantage of the voltage fluctuations that persisted in Kerala during those times and invested in massive production of stabilizers and fresh products, including inverters. Slowly but surely, V-Guard's market expanded to neighbouring states. His sons Arun and Mithun, currently Managing Directors of Wonderla and V-Guard respectively, joined him in due course. Soon V-Guard also conquered the markets beyond South India.

Kochouseph Chittilappilly with the former President of India A.P.J.Abdul Kalam

FAMILY MAN

Kochouseph, born to doting parents, knew the importance of family life. So despite his busy schedule, he always found time to spend with his family. Be it going to amusement parks or travels abroad, Kochouseph made it a point to take the family along. Taking inspiration from these trips, Kochouseph started an amusement park named Veegaland in Kochi. In 2000, it was opened for the public and after five years, he was ready with another amusement park called Wonderla in Bengaluru. Later, Veegaland was merged into the brand name Wonderla. In 2016, a branch of Wonderla was opened in Hyderabad.

As an entrepreneur, Kochouseph Chittilappilly always believed in transparency. Keen that his employees brought their best to the workplace, he listed both the companies on the stock exchange and gave employees 5% shares of his company. The move created a sense of responsibility and commitment amongst them. He sharpened the skills of his employees and gave them more perks and responsibilities, adding professionalism to his company while safeguarding its status.

Two beliefs propelled Kochouseph throughout his life: practical knowledge is more important than academics, and a skilled businessman is a multi-tasker. His multifaceted management, business, and technical skills have been applauded by many, and aptly so. An epitome of success, Kochouseph Chittilappilly will continue to inspire generations of entrepreneurs to come.

KOCHOUSEPH CHITTILAPPILLY

Kochouseph Chittilappilly's inspiring story begins in the modest suburbs of Parappur in Thrissur. He was born in a middle-class family in 1950. Despite his family's farming background, he rose to become a recognised name in the industrial arena with the crown-jewel of his accomplishments – V-Guard Industries. Kochouseph owns a chain of amusement parks called Wonderla Holidays Limited and heads Veegaland Developers, the real estate arm. He was given the Government of India's Highest Individual Income Taxpayer Award after 17 years of V-Guard's successful journey. Kochouseph debuted on Forbes' Billionaires list 2018 with a net worth of $1.2 billion. With a donaton of Rs. 22 crore, he has been ranked by Hurun as the 37th most generous Indian in 2021 Hurun India Philanthorpy List.

As an entrepreneur, he received many honors and awards for his top-notch services. But even after building a mighty business empire, he remains connected to his humble roots. As a philanthropist, he actively involves in various social works through his charitable trust K. Chittilappilly Foundation (KCF). He is a strong campaigner of cadaver donation and has donated one of his kidneys to an anonymous person. His books Practical Wisdom, Ormakilivathil, Ormakalilekku Oru Yatra, and The Gift and Journey towards Hope give accounts of his priceless experiences.

9

AZAD THE BENEVOLENT

Azad was the youngest of seven children. His father, Ahmed Unni Moopen, was a freedom fighter, farmer, and merchant. Born in prosperous times, Azad was lovingly called 'Bava' by family members. When enrolled at school, a teacher asked for his name during the registration process, to which he replied, "Azad." Unlike most children, he had the opportunity to choose his name. Thus Azad Moopen ventured out in a special way to become a tall entrepreneur-cum-doctor in modern medicine.

As the youngest son, Azad was pampered by his father. He taught the young boy multiplication. Azad went on to excel in Math. Unni Moopen relied on him for accounting in their businesses. Azad also had the task of reading out the newspaper loud for his father. So the little boy grew up well informed about world events. When the students of Kalpakanchery Govt. High School went on a strike, Azad, who was in the seventh standard, joined them. After this incident, his father, a respected figure in society, 'deported' him to Kozhikode.

Azad studied at St. Joseph's Boys High School from the eighth standard onwards. It became a turning point in his life. The new environment opened doors to a world outside of Kalpakanchery, and he gained English proficiency here. His father passed away when he was in the tenth standard. He wished his son to become a doctor, and Azad was bent on realising that dream.

Dr.Azad Moopen and his wife Nazeera, with their
children Ziham, Alisha and Dr. Zeba

He joined Farook College, Kozhikode, to pursue the Pre-Degree course. Political inclination hadn't deserted him yet, and he joined the Students Federation of India (SFI) here. Azad's low marks meant he wouldn't get an MBBS seat. Hence he enrolled at the same college for his bachelor's. His impressive score in the bachelor's degree secured him an MBBS seat at Kozhikode Medical College. He became a hero of sorts after leading a strike against the decision to include students of homeopathy at the medical college. He took an MD in General Medicine from the same college and then became a teacher there. Azad later enrolled for higher studies at Delhi University.

His social activities, in the meantime, continued. A fundraising activity for a local institution took him to the UAE with friends. There he met Dr. Ali, who, incidentally, was looking for a doctor to run his clinic in Ajman, close to Dubai. He invited Dr. Azad Moopen to his clinic.

After mulling over the offer for a while, he took leave from Kozhikode Medical College for five years and flew to Dubai. In 1987, Dr. Moopen started his new innings at Dr. Ali's clinic in Ajman. Dr. Ali advised Moopen to move to Dubai, where, with his abilities, he can run his own clinic. But Moopen, who had flown down to give Dr. Ali a hand for a few years, could not even think of a long-term commitment such as running his own clinic. At Dr. Ali's insistence, he finally gave in and started a small clinic called Al Rafa on the ground floor of a flat complex in Dubai in December. There began Dr. Azad Moopen's entrepreneurial journey to setting up Aster DM Healthcare, a vast hospital network that provides healthcare to countless patients in India and the Gulf.

It didn't take long for patients from Dubai to come seeking the advice of the doctor who was already popular in India. A majority of them were low-income workers from Kerala. Soon, he was busy attending to patients from 8 am to midnight. With every passing day, the patient flow increased, touching 100-120 numbers per day. More doctors were appointed to manage the numbers. At the end of each passing year, Moopen thought he would return permanently to his hometown. But in the meantime, the doctor and family began to love Dubai, their new dream city. After five years, he started another clinic in Dubai and a pharmacy with it. The growth in the number of clinics was prolific, each with a different name. Some of the clinics failed to cause a setback, but Moopen was not one to be deterred. He used every lesson as a stepping stone to forge new paths.

Each time he was in town on vacation, Dr. Moopen thought that Malabar could have a hospital providing quality treatment. At that time, many people from Malabar travelled to neighbouring states for treatment. Soon Dr. Azad Moopen established MIMS at Kozhikode in 2001. Many like-minded people joined him in realising it. Providing top-quality treatment, MIMS brought back many Malayali doctors working abroad. A scheme was launched to treat those from the lower strata of society setting apart five percent of the total profit of MIMS. Moopen was also ready with money for the hospital's development whenever necessary.

In 2007, India Value Fund Advisors (IVFA), a prominent private equity firm came onboard with capital investment. The company acquired 26 percent shares of MIMS at a valuation of Rs. 450 Crore. The company began to grow by leaps and bounds with the fund pumping. In 2010, all hospitals and clinics came under a single brand called 'Aster.' MIMS too became an affiliate of Aster DM Healthcare. The hospital network was strengthened in India as well.

Dr.Azad Moopen with former President of India A.P.J.Abdul Kalam

In 2012, another private equity firm Olympus Capital arrived on the scene with an investment of Rs.500 Crore. The investment was made at a valuation of Rs.1800 Crore. Today Aster DM has more than 370 hospitals, clinics, and pharmacies in India, U.A.E, Qatar, Oman, Bahrain, Saudi Arabia, Jordan, and the Philippines. Apart from Kozhikode Aster MIMS, Kottakkal Aster MIMS, Kannur Aster MIMS, and Kochi Aster Medcity, the group also controls the operations of the hospital at Wayanad DM WIMS Medical College. Plans are afoot for a 600-bed multispeciality hospital near Akkulam in Thiruvananthapuram. Aster also has presence in Karnataka, Andhra Pradesh, Telangana, and Maharashtra. Two more hospitals are being set up in Bengaluru and one in Chennai.

Aster DM Healthcare currently employs over 20,000 people in the Gulf, India, and the Philippines. This includes 3,000 doctors and 6,500 nurses. The group provides healthcare to 50,000 people every day. Today, Moopen's enterprise has grown into one of the largest healthcare networks in India and the Gulf. In February 2018, Aster DM Healthcare raised Rs 980 Crore through an Initial Public Offering (IPO). After the IPO, Aster has become the third-largest hospital network in India in terms of market value.

The lessons that Dr. Moopen learned over three decades of his entrepreneurial life are varied. He recalls what his youngest daughter Dr. Zeba said after attending a couple of meetings at Aster. "Most of the meetings were about healthcare, patients, and illnesses earlier. But now, discussions are only about the number of crores," she said. Dr. Moopen says that his daughters' words gave him deep insight, prompting him to ensure the presence of doctors at important meetings. Suggestions to improve the quality and safety aspects of healthcare began to gain prominence in the meetings. Profit is only a by-product in the healthcare business. According to Moopen, thoughts and insights emerge when we listen. Dr.Moopen considers his experience in student politics and as an academician as a great asset in his entrepreneurial life.

He says while business was ingrained in his DNA, he didn't set out to become an entrepreneur, "When opportunities knock on the door, one should not consider it as a burden. All you have to do is open the door and welcome those opportunities." He believes that luck, hard work, and teamwork are essential elements for success on the entrepreneurial path. Ever keen to uplift the poor, Dr. Azad Moopen has set aside 20 percent of his wealth for charitable activities under Dr. Moopen's Foundation and Aster DM Foundation. On the group's 30th anniversary in 2017, all these activities were brought under Aster Volunteers. Paying back to the roots, the family runs the Moopen's Institute for Local Empowerment (MILES), a local empowerment programme in Kalpakanchery.

DR. AZAD MOOPEN

Dr. Azad Moopen, Founder Chairman and Managing Director of Aster DM Healthcare, is a popular name in healthcare across India and the Middle East. He was born in 1953 in Kalpakanchery near Tirur, Malappuram district, to Ahmed Unni Moopen and Ayesha, a member of the Kalliyath family. The Hurun India Rich List 2021 valued his wealth at Rs.4,900 crore.

He is one of the Directors of NORKA ROOTS and President of the NORKA Department Project for Returned Emigrants (NDPREM). He was a member of the Governing Council of Kerala University of Health Sciences (KUHS). Dr. Azad was also on the Board of Directors of Kerala State Coastal Area Development Corporation (KSCADC).

In 2009, he received the Best Doctor Award from the Government of Kerala and the Arab Health Award from the Arab Health Forum in 2010. The country honoured him with Pravasi Bharatiya Samman in 2010 and the Padma Shri in 2011.

Dr. Azad is married to Nazeera Azad. They have three children: Alisha (Chartered Accountant cum Deputy Managing Director, Aster DM Healthcare), Ziham (Managing Director, Toddler Town British Nursery, Dubai), and Dr. Zeba (Director, Aster DM Healthcare).

10

FRAGRANCE OF DESTINY

A person who is among the first to explore or settle in a new country or area - that's how the Oxford English Dictionary defines 'pioneer.' C.V. Jacob, who founded Synthite Industries, one of the top industrial units to extract value-added products from spices, was a pioneer who explored unchartered territories. He is also among the first-generation visionary entrepreneurs from Kerala. C.V. Jacob is the first entrepreneur in Kerala to spot the possibilities of oleoresins common in the West. He set up Synthite Industries at Kolenchery, a non-descript village in Ernakulam, in 1972.

Jacob started his aromatic journey at an early age. Shortly after school, he established a cardamom business. His sister's husband, E.J. Paulose, who ran a cardamom plantation close-by, was his mentor.

After a brief stint in the cardamom business, Jacob followed in the footsteps of his father, C.U. Varkey, in the construction contract business. With his elder brother C.V. John, Jacob bagged the tender for undertaking concrete works for the Chenkulam tunnel in 1953. In the subsequent years, he single-handedly constructed what is known as the 'jeep road' associated with the Kallarkutty Hydro Electric project. After that, Jacob completed the Kallarkutty Bridge, the tunnel of the Anayirankal dam, and the Upper Kallar project. Later he undertook many constructions related to the Pamba, Kakki, Moolamattom, Idukki, and Cheruthoni dams. He also undertook part of the construction works of the Kochi-Cherthala National Highway stretch.

C.V.Jacob receiving National Export Award 1984-85 from the then
President of India R.Venkataraman

A freak accident in which a boulder fell on his brother-in-law Paulose during the construction of Moolamattom Dam in 1966, leading to his death, traumatised Jacob, and he left the field for good. He organised his men from the construction business to start a new venture, 'Slabs and Aggregates,' for producing metals by crushing rocks. The first fully-equipped crushing unit in Kerala, it met the metal demand in Kerala. Even as he faced protests from several trade unions, Jacob held his ground.

The aggressive entrepreneur in Jacob established another industrial unit, Arboritis, at Petta near Tripunithura in 1965. It innovatively made glue by hewing plywood. A Japanese company that supplied raw materials for this industry invited Jacob to participate in the International Trade Expo in 1970. It impacted a career shift for Jacob.

Entrepreneurs from different countries showed up at the 'Expo Japan 70' fest. His interactions with other participants helped him learn more about other business possibilities. Promptly he turned to the field of oleoresins.

Someone already exposed to spices, he instantly identified its business possibilities. No one at the fair was willing to reveal the alchemy behind the extraction process, but they offered to sell him the product. A third party taking the spices from our backyard only to sell the final product to the same people infuriated Jacob to no end. He was sure that this strategy would not sustain itself in the long run.

The newfound possibility lingered on Jacob's mind even after returning from Japan. He then chanced upon a newspaper report on oleoresins. It specified that the Central Food Technological Research Institute (CFTRI), Bangalore, was technically equipped for oleoresin extraction. He set off to Bangalore right away to understand the method. The institute agreed to part with the technology for producing oleoresins for a royalty percentage from his returns.

Hopeful of realizing his dream, Jacob launched his company. The enterprise was christened Synthite Industrial Chemicals Limited. a name he had initially reserved for other projects. The first contract involved extracting oleoresin from the pepper. With this, Synthite became the first oleoresins manufacturer from Kerala.

Meanwhile, Dr. K.P. George, a relative of C.V. Jacob based in America, confirmed the immense marketing potential of the product there. He spotted a New York-based company interested in purchasing oleoresins.

The US company struck a deal as soon as they visited the Synthite factory. But they placed a condition - Synthite should not sell oleoresins to any other company in the US; if Synthite wanted to sell to a third party, it would have to be through them. Jacob agreed. The US firm was also ready to provide technical assistance. The first export consignment worth Rs.60,000 went out, creating a breakthrough.

Huge primary capital and raw materials were required for oleoresin production. Jacob sought bank loans, but the applications were rejected. Later, an official who was his acquaintance helped get the loan by pawning the raw materials.

With its first export, Synthite entered the road to success. There was a spurt in the number of products and subsidiaries soon. Factories came up in China and different states in India. Jacob set up factories in Ongole in Andhra Pradesh, famous for its red chilies, and Tamil Nadu to extract flower essences, ensuring a consistent raw material supply. In due course, Synthite started dominating one-third of the global oleoresins trade.

C.V.Jacob with his wife Eliyamma

In addition to extracting oleoresins, Synthite started manufacturing natural compounds for adding scent, taste, and colour to food items. Many soft drinks and food manufacturing multinationals turned clients of Synthite. The company then introduced curry powders and masala powders under the brand Kitchen Treasures. Synthite also made strides in real estate and hospitality by developing Riviera Retreat in Kochi and Ramada Resorts in Kumbalam.

In addition to his children and their spouses, Jacob's nephew George Paul also joined the business. At Synthite, employees were treated like family. Gifts and bonuses were awarded to employees who completed a certain period of service in the company. As of now, more than 2,500 employees work directly at Synthite, and 25,000 indirectly.

C.V. Jacob, always the pioneer, showed keen interest when Cochin International Airport in Nedumbassery emerged as a PPP enterprise. He was one of the first to join the drive to raise capital for the project, contributing Rs 25 lakh. He was also made Director of the airport quite early.

He has made commendable contributions to society, actively establishing institutions such as St. Peter's College, Kolenchery, St. Peter's School, Kadayiruppu, Mar Baselios Engineering College, Kolenchery, MOSC Medical College, Kolencherry, and so on. The CVJ Foundation is actively involved in social activities. Jacob imbibed many qualities in his 60-year-old business odessey, the most important being the willingness to experiment with novel initiatives.

C.V. JACOB

C.V. Jacob, Founder and Former Chairman of Synthite Industries, the largest oleoresins company in the world, has left behind an ambrosial aroma that he created from scratch. He has received the Central Government-instituted Best Exporter Award several times from 1976-77, apart from several other prestigious national and international awards.

Born at Nechupadam House, Kolenchery, on September 27, 1933, as the son of prominent contractor C.U.Varkey and Eli, C.V. Jacob married Eliyamma, a member of the Meppadam family. They have six children, Dr. Viju Jacob, Aju Jacob, Elvy, Silvy, Minna, and Minni. C.V. Jacob passed away on January 31, 2021.

11

THE 'MUHAMMA SOFTWARE'

In 1980, a young lad from Muhamma, in Alappuzha district, was hired as an engineer by Patni Computer Systems Limited, one of the first software companies in India. It happened at a time when the world around him was not familiar with what the job entailed. Right from the beginning, unparalleled sincerity to his work remained the hallmark of S.D. Shibulal.

It is what catapulted his career to dizzying heights over the years. While at Patni, Shibulal reported to N.R. Narayana Murthy. On one such occasion, Shibulal went to Murthy to submit a periodic progress report on the software that he was working on. The latter was preoccupied with his work and asked him to return home only after completing his work. Two days later, when Murthy dropped by the office at midnight to collect some documents he had forgotten, he saw Shibulal hunched over his work, wearing a lungi (an ethnic informal garment worn around the waist by men in some parts of India). Needless to say, Murthy was bemused but impressed over his sincerity.

Around this time, Murthy was mulling over starting his own IT firm. He extended an invitation to Shibulal, and the latter ended up being one of the seven founding members of Infosys along with Murthy.

Shibulal was drawn to science quite early. He found great joy in discovering, understanding, and creating things. Both his parents supported their only son in pursuing his interests. After completing his high school education from T.D. Higher Secondary School, he joined S.D. College, Alappuzha, for Pre-Degree and then Maharaja's College, Ernakulam, for the degree. Shibulal followed them with a postgraduation in M.Sc. Physics from S.N College, Kollam. Then a period of uncertainty crept in, leaving him on a job hunt. The wandering led him to Mumbai, where he got his first job at Bombay Electric Supply and Transport (B.E.S.T) as a programmer. Even though he did not benefit much monetarily, the living quarters provided by the organization came as a huge relief.

B.E.S.T ran the famous red buses. Shibulal was in charge of developing a proper ticketing system for B.E.S.T using modern technology. It was a challenge as the young man was yet to come across a computer. He used to write programmes on a coding sheet. Around this time, the Tata Institute of Fundamental Research (TIFR) started a Computer Science course. Determined to gain the required know-how, Shibulal joined the course, dividing his days between work and studies. It was here that he got first-hand exposure to computer systems.

By the time he joined Patni Computer Systems in 1979, he had two years of work experience at B.E.S.T. He joined as a software engineer at his new workplace. Patni changed the course of his career, especially after his bonding with N.R. Narayana Murthy. Shibulal's proficiency in COBOL and Assembly programming made him an invaluable asset to Murthy's startup initiative.

Initially, Shibulal felt it a risk to throw away a perfect job. But second thoughts prompted him to believe that there wouldn't be any dearth of opportunities in the new field. Finally, in 1981, seven engineers, including Shibulal and Murthy, resigned from Patni computers to start their own company Infosys - all seven belonged to middle-class families having no business background. Murthy's idea was to bag foreign software contracts and deal with the clients' needs from India. Initially, the company acted as a subcontracting agency for Data Basics Corporation based in New York.

S.D.Shibulal, and wife Kumari Shibulal with renowned physicist Stephen Hawking

In the initial stage, Shibulal moved to Florida to work as the project manager of the company. He had pawned his wife's jewellery for buying his share in the company. By the time, fortunately, the firm started growing. Later he shifted from Florida to Boston and began working on a contract for Reebok. Meanwhile, in 1983, the Infosys headquarters was moved from Pune to Bangalore.

In 1987, Infosys got its first exclusive client, Digital Equipment Corporation (DEC), a Boston-based company. Infosys started to thrive, overcoming the initial hiccups. In the same year, the company tied up with KSA, a management consultancy group from the US. It seemed a great step forward for the company, but the association shook its very foundation. One of the co-founders, Ashok Arora, chose to leave the company. But Murthy declared that the enterprise would continue to work as it did before. The rest of the board members, including Shibulal, stood by him. Then on, it was a rise to the top for Infosys.

In 1991, with the consent of fellow board members, Shibulal took a short break from the company. He joined Sun Microsystems, an American technology company, for two years. Later he extended this stint for two more years.

Shibulal was assigned the task of developing an e-commerce platform for Sun Microsystems. The time he spent as project manager for Reebok and Sun Microsystems stood him in good stead in this phase. Sun Microsystems gave him a better understanding of the Internet that revolutionised the tech space.

In 1993, Infosys came out with its Initial Public Offering (IPO). Shares ranging from Rs.10 to Rs.95 were put up for sale. Not many investors showed interest initially, but Infosys managed to sell all their shares successfully after a short lag. Later the company created history on the stock market by ramping up more than enough investments.

S.D.Shibulal (extreme right) with Infosys co- founder N.R.Narayana Murthy and his early colleagues

By 1997, Shibulal resigned from Sun Microsystems to dive headlong back into Infosys again. He started an Internet Consultancy Practices Department in the company. It catapulted Infosys into one of the world's largest service providers in business consultancy and IT services. Soon, he also headed the International Sales Department of the company.

In 2007, he was anointed the Chief Operating Officer (COO) of the company. On August 21, 2011, he was promoted to Managing Director and Chief Executive Officer. Finally, on July 31, 2014, just seven months before his retirement, he resigned from the post of CEO. But this was after he helped spiral the company's annual turnover to Rs. 50,000 Crore.

Post-retirement, he started Axilor Ventures with another Infosys co-founder, Kris Gopalakrishnan. Axilor Ventures stepped in to help promising startup entrepreneurs. Some of his colleagues from Infosys, like Srinath Batni, Ganapathy Venugopal, and Tarun Khanna (also a professor of Harvard University), became a part of this initiative. Based in Bangalore, Axilor provides seed money for new startup enterprises.

Shibulal also created Innovation Investment Management India Private Limited, which functions as his family office, and using the firm, he invests in various business ventures. Shibulal is part of the Tamara Resort, founded by his daughter Shruti Shibulal. He undertakes education, health, and social welfare activities through the Sarojini Damodaran Foundation and the Advaith Foundation.

While Shibulal swears by hard work, commitment, and dedication to achieving professional success, he also believes luck plays an important role. He firmly believes that staying true to your beliefs and values is essential even when you pass through different phases.

"Ideas are important for budding businesses, but success lies in the proper execution of these ideas. Building a business is definitely not easy. It is like a marathon. It takes time," Shibulal reminds all aspiring entrepreneurs. "What you have achieved is just as important as how you achieve it. It is important not to compromise on your values and ethics. Businesses should have good leadership." As a final piece of advice, Shibulal asks budding entrepreneurs to seek help and guidance from experienced entrepreneurs when needed.

S.D. SHIBULAL

S.D. Shibulal is the co-founder of India's second-largest IT firm Infosys. He served as the company's Managing Director and Chief Executive Officer (CEO) from 2011 to 2014. He was born in 1955 in Muhamma, a small village in Alappuzha district, Kerala. His father, C.K. Damodaran, was an Ayurvedic doctor and his mother, Sarojini, was an Excise Department employee.

After completing his school and college education in Kerala, he took MS in Computer Science from Boston University. Shibulal is now a member of the board of trustees of Boston University. He also serves as a member of the state advisory board of Kerala IT. He holds memberships in various other global forums and consultative boards. He co-founded Axilor Ventures, a platform that supports upcoming entrepreneurs, and is the Chairman of Tamara Resorts, a hospitality venture owned by his daughter Shruti Shibulal. The Hurun India Rich List values S.D. Shibulal's wealth at Rs. 17,700 Crore and with a donaton of Rs. 35 Crore, he has been ranked by Hurun as the 23rd most generous Indian in 2021 Hurun India Philanthorpy List.

He is married to Kumari, a patron and founding member of Sarojini Damodaran Foundation (founded in 1999) and Advaith Foundation (founded in 2004). The couple has two children: Shruti Shibulal, an MBA-holder from Columbia University and currently Managing Director of The Tamara Resorts and Shreyas Shibulal, an MS-holder in Computer Science from the University of Pennsylvania and currently Founder of Micelio Mobility.

12

THE GOLDEN TOUCH

M.P. Ahammed was the only son of Arikkulath Mammed Kutty Haji and Pathumma couple, who had five sisters. Kutty Haji was a farmer and a merchant who never let his children know the hardships of life. Ahammed, too, grew up free from any responsibilities. But destiny had other plans, as it thrust upon the 24-year-old Ahammed's shoulders the burden of his family when Kutty Haji died. Life began to reveal harsh realities, one after another. In 1981, Ahmed moved to Kozhikode town. He joined a merchant in the copra business. Within a short time, the youngster won the trust of his clients, and many expressed interest in partnering with him. They respected his transparency in money matters. In 1982, Ahammed started his own copra business named Syndicate in Kozhikode town by pooling public contributions, the fortune he received by selling his family property, and the money he raised by selling pepper grown at home.

His friend, a transport agent, helped Ahammed to send copra to North India. Ahammed earned the trust of the farmers by getting them the best prices. Ahammed was everyone's choice to do business with. While Syndicate saw its fortune going up, the young man did not confine to just trading in copra. He began to explore the gold trade possibilities. He spent time with some jewellers to get a better understanding of the industry. Meanwhile, his sisters' grownup children joined Ahammed in business.

In 1993, Malabar Gold began to operate out of a 700 square feet space on the top floor of Colombo Complex at Palayam, Kozhikode.

It was a thoroughly experimental venture with a start-up capital of Rs 50 lakh. The business was named 'Malabar' as most of its investors were non-resident Malayalis from the Malabar region.

M.P.Ahammed and his wife Subaida with their family

Old habits die hard, so people were unwilling to shop at the new shop in town. They were used to visiting traditional gold merchants, but gradually change set in. Despite the showroom being on the top floor of the building, not offering the best visibility, more customers began to step in. From day one, Ahammed's emphasis was on providing top-quality gold and courteous service to patrons. He also understood the need to strengthening marketing efforts. Soon, Ahammed and his group approached a prominent Malayalam film personality with a proposal to make him the brand ambassador of Malabar Gold. The actor asked them to come back after changing the company's name, but Ahammed was unrelenting. Years later, in 2004, film icon Mohanlal became its brand ambassador, marking his debut as the brand ambassador of a jewellery brand. The advertisement campaign with the tagline 'Atmabandhathinte

Suvarna Sparsham,' meaning 'The golden touch of a soulful relation,' quickly resonated among Malayalis. Malabar Gold pioneered the 'Brand Ambassador Culture' in Kerala by roping in movie stars for their advertisements. Mohanlal set the ball rolling, with a galaxy of stars including Sania Mirza, Hema Malini, Ilayaraja, NTR Jr., Puneet Rajkumar, Kareena Kapoor, Suriya, Kajal Aggarwal, Tamanna, Manushi Chillar, Anil Kapoor and now Karthi following suit for Malabar Gold.

By 2000, Malabar Gold shifted to its own building in Kozhikode city, and a hotel and shopping complex under the brand name Malabar Gate was added to the Malabar Group. Ahammed turned all his attention to the jewellery enterprise from the copra business. New showrooms were opened at Tirur and Kannur; rather, the group acquired two failed jewellery businesses and relaunched them under the Malabar Gold brand name.

Malabar Gold's assurance of quality and reliability ensured it a solid customer base. The attention to building good personal relationships with the customers also won them their loyalty. Malabar Gold seemed destined to grow beyond Malabar. The brand put its stamp on major cities in South India - Bengaluru, Chennai, and Hyderabad. Then it goose-stepped into North India. The business tapped into different kinds of customer bases, offering them ethnic ornaments. Following detailed research, wedding ornaments were launched under the brand 'Brides of India.'

In 2003, heeding the call of the Arab soil, a showroom was opened in Dubai. But the showroom had to be closed down in two years after facing losses. The group took stock of the situation and found that the magic of Malabar Group was missing in Dubai. They discovered that the wrong location, insufficient supply, and lack of advertising contributed to the failure. In 2008, Malabar Gold made a grand re-entry to the Gulf. This time, it quickly gained prominence as an international brand in the retail jewellery segment. Malabar Gold could establish 100 showrooms overall in just two decades of its launch. In 2013, the hundredth showroom was inaugurated in Gurgaon, near Delhi.

Today, Malabar Gold and Diamonds has 260 showrooms in 10 countries including UAE, Bahrain, Qatar, Kuwait, Oman, Saudi Arabia, Singapore, Malaysia, and the US. It could spread out wings with new investors coming on board, including Non-Resident Entrepreneurs, celebrities, and employees of Malabar Gold itself. Breaking boundaries of religion, caste, and language, the brand has a base of 4000 investors worldwide.

M.P.Ahammed receiving CSR Award from Sheikh Ahmed bin Saeed Al Maktoum, President, Dubai Civil Aviation Authority and Chairman of Emirates Airline Group

By now, there was no stopping for Ahammed, who stepped into the real estate sector with Malabar Developers. The first three projects met with losses. As always, he learned from his mistakes. Malabar Developers now has several residential complexes across Kerala, along with townships and shopping malls. There are projects in other parts of India too.

Malabar Group now has divisions for jewellery-making and wholesale. The group also has an electronics and home appliances retail chain, Eham, and a luxury watches division, Malabar Watches. Malabar Group is now a noble venture of promoting organic farming in the State of Kerala.

Ahammed faced a fair share of predicaments in his journey as an entrepreneur. While the Malabar Group was in its nascent stages, it launched Malabar Silks but failed to make an impact. Ahammed was smart and retreated from the textile business, gauging it was not his forte. Their failed first attempt in the Gulf was also a lesson learned the hard way. Addressing its shortcomings, the Malabar Group staged powerful comebacks. Today, Malabar Gold has grown to become one of the largest jewellery groups in the world. The Malabar Group is a corporate house with an annual turnover of Rs.30,000 Crore and an employee strength of around 13,000 men and women.

M P. Ahammed always understood real-time trends in business and the economy. As an entrepreneur, he was always keen to share a part of his success with the lower strata of society. He has been keeping aside a fixed share of profits for giving a hand to the less fortunate. These humanitarian efforts are carried out under the Malabar Charitable Trust. Five per cent of company's profit has been earmarked for charity and a team has been tasked to spend the funds effectively. Housing, health services, scholarships for girls, and gold assets for economically backward girls are provided through the programme 'Golden Heart'. The trust is also into activities of environmental protection.

Ahammed believes that transparency can build relationships, helping the business grow. He is proof that only those who learn from their mistakes can succeed as entrepreneurs. "Business should be considered as a service. One should do business with a commitment to society," he says.

Malabar Group is fully committed to transparency in business, in that sense he is swimming against the current. Ahammed has introduced 'One India, One Gold Rate' a year ago and levies same price in all the shops throughout the country. His concept, 'Make in India, Market to the World' has received great attention and appreciation even from Govt. of India. He has great plans to augment jewellery manufacturing in India and export to different countries.

M.P. AHAMMED

Malabar Gold & Diamonds needs no introduction. As a brand, it has gone on to capture hearts in a short time. M.P. Ahammed, Founder and Chairman of the retail jewellery group, was born in 1957 to Arikulam Mammed Kutty Haji and Pathumma of Koyilandy in Kozhikode.

He is the General Secretary of the Kerala Jewellers Federation, a collective of large jewellery groups in Kerala. He has received several awards, including the Bombay Bullion Association and the Times Group Global Jeweller awards.

Ahammed is married to Subaida, and the couple has two children, Shamlal Ahmed (Managing Director, International Operations, Malabar Group) and Soujat Ashar, married to Ashni and Ashar (Managing Director, India Operations, Malabar Group), respectively.

13

A SQUEAKY-CLEAN MERCHANT

All it takes is colours to light up one's world. But this commoner from Thrissur chose white for his signature look. Yes, this is none other than Moothedath Panjan Ramachandran – the humble founder of Jyothy Labs, one of India's largest FMCG companies.

The mastermind behind 'Chaar boondon wala Ujala' does not have a great beginning to his story. He was born in a middle-class peasant family in Kandanassery. Just like any other boy, he dreamt of becoming a doctor someday. After schooling in Kandanassery and Mattathu, he joined the Pre-Degree course with science as his main in Guruvayur Sree Krishna College. Unfortunately, he did not fare well and had to give up his dream of becoming a doctor, joining BCom at St. Thomas College, Thrissur, instead.

He went to Kolkata soon after to join a cost accountant intermediate course. In 1971, Ramachandran moved to Mumbai and started working in an educational film production company. He later quit and started working as an accountant at a chemical company, for a monthly wage of Rs. 150. Ramachandran worked there for 12 years but at the same time pursued a postgraduate degree in financial management at the University of Bombay. Meanwhile, he got married and moved into a small flat in Mumbai with his wife.

The chemical company he worked, got embroiled in a major crisis leading to its shutdown in 1981. Still, Ramachandran continued with the job to settle the accounts there. However, he had his future in mind and was convinced that he should be an entrepreneur. While working at the chemical company, Ramachandran found it challenging to maintain his white clothes spotless, something he had practised emulating his father. After washing, soaps and detergents left marks on clothes too. Ramachandran mulled the possibilities of a solution that would do away with these marks and asked himself why he couldn't start such a business. He discussed the idea with a few other chemists and decided to head back to Thrissur.

In 1983, with his meagre life-savings of Rs. 5000, Ramachandran opened a small-scale unit named 'Jyothy Labs' after his daughter and introduced his product Ujala to the market: the brand promised spotless white clothes to its customers. A new product aimed at easing the workload of housemakers by quickly dissolving in water, Ujala did not leave any stains on the clothes. However, a few months later, the company inched towards closing down as the product wasn't picking up in the market. But destiny had other plans. One fine morning he received an order from a distributor in Malappuram for 1000 Ujala bottles. From there, Ujala reared its head again. He shifted production to his father's place in Kandanassery. Business boomed with sales touching Rs 40,000 in the first year.

Despite soaring sales, packaging ate into the cost as the bottles did not come cheap. Luckily, Ramachandran's former boss came to his rescue with a piece of timely advice to sell Ujala in plastic bottles. It helped the company cut the packaging cost by over 50 percent, making sales more profitable. The company picked up rapidly. By 1987, the product entered the Tamil Nadu market. Ramachandran started advertising his products in newspapers and magazines. Soon, Ujala's catchy jingle 'Chaar boondon wala' caught up on the radio.

M.P.Ramachandran with Ullas Kamath, former Joint Managing Director,
Jyothy Labs

By 1988, the turnover of the company touched Rs. 1 Crore. Soon Ramachandran's prized business was caught in the perils of unhealthy competition, with many counterfeit products surfacing in the market. His company was raided multiple times and slapped with enormous fines. But Ramachandran's honesty saw him through it all. The counterfeit products never made it too far. Jyothy Labs, meanwhile, moved with the times, diversifying with multiple brands and expanding its marketing and brand-building strategy. Products crossed borders to the Middle East and other Asian and Western nations. Later, the company set up a factory in Bangladesh and a big one in Thrissur.

From the very beginning, Jyothi Lab provided family pension and provident fund to the workers. In 1993, he established a new factory in Chennai and another one in Pondicherry within two years. Ramachandran introduced a washing soap called Nebula into the market in 1995. But following the imposition of a 12 percent tax, he stopped producing the soap as it failed to reap enough profit. Ujala flourished across the Indian market and had a turnover of Rs 100 crore in 1999.

Meanwhile, Barings Investments, an investment arm of the global financial institution ING Group, made a capital investment in Jyothy Labs, taking a 10 percent stake. In 2002, they sold it to CDC and CLSA Global private equity firms for a huge profit. Recognising the growth potential of Jyothy Labs, investors increased their stake to 30 percent. They then held a public issue in 2007 to sell their shares. With this, the shares of Jyothy Labs started trending on the Bombay Stock Exchange and the National Stock Exchange.

M.P.Ramachandran with Pinarayi Vijayan, Chief Minister of Kerala

Jyothy Labs did not stop diversification with the Nebula fiasco. In 2000, mosquito repellent products were launched in the market under the brand name Maxo. Jyothy Labs also launched other products like Vanamala Washing Soap, Maya Agarbati, Jeeva Ayurvedic Soap, Exo Dishwash, Ujala Stiff & Shine, and Ujala Techno Bright Detergent. Today, Ujala leads the fabric whitener market nationally, with a market share of about 78 percent. Ujala is available across price points – from Rs. 1 to Rs 45 –

for individuals across the consumption curve. Exo ranks second in the dishwash bar market, while Maxo has a strong presence in the mosquito-control product market.

In 2011, Jyothy Labs acquired a 50.9 percent stake in the 30-year-old Henkel India – the Indian subsidiary of the German-based Henkel company. Jyothy Labs attained an excellent portfolio with Henkel, which has brands like Pril, Margo, Henko, and Fa. Jyothy Labs' strong R&D team enhanced the quality of every Henkel product. With this, the sales of these brands started to flourish. After taking over Henkel, Jyothy Labs' annual turnover in 2011 crossed Rs. 1,000 crore. In addition to Jyothy Labs, the group also owns a laundry company called Jyothy Fabricare Services. Its fabric-spa chain, which flourished in Mumbai and Bengaluru, now has an outlet at Delhi airport. The Indian Railways and many hotel chains are major customers of Jyothy Fabricare Services.

Within three-and-a-half decades, Jyothy Labs has become a company with a market value of Rs. 6,000 Crore. More than 5,000 staff work at the company which has an annual turnover of around Rs. 2,000 Crore. The group has more than 30 factories in different parts of the country. Ullas Kamath, the joint managing director of Jyothy Labs, has been a strong pillar of support to Ramachandran for almost three decades. Ramachandran retired from the post of managing director and handed over the reins to his elder daughter M.R.Jyothy on April 1, 2020. Ramachandran continues to serve as the Chairman Emeritus of the company.

Ramachandran aims to make Jyothy Labs the number one FMCG company in India. His entrepreneurial journey has been fraught with many battles. He feels: "Every challenge is a step towards growth. A true entrepreneur faces failures with courage." He adds that one should be able to find the right opportunity from the options available.

M.P. RAMACHANDRAN

M.P. Ramachandran was born in 1946 to Moothedathuveetil Panjan and Valliamma at Kandanassery in Thrissur. He is the Founder and Chairman Emiretus of Jyothy Labs Ltd., one of India's largest Fast Moving Consumer Goods (FMCG) companies. After retiring from Jyothy Labs, Ramachandran launched Amrut Veni range of hair care products under a new entity called Sahyadri Bio Labs.

Ramachandran was honoured with various awards like the P.V. Sami Memorial Award and Times Group Brand Icon Award. He is also involved in several social welfare activities. Ramachandran is married to Santhakumari. Of their daughters, Jyothy took over as the Managing Director of the company in April 2020, and Deepthi controls the finance department. His sons-in-law Anand Rao heads operations and Ravi Rasdan the IT-HR department.

14

PANACEA MAN

A Malayali heads Strides Pharma Science Limited, a Bangalore-based leading Indian pharma company. Arun Kumar, a native of Kavanadu, Kollam, who runs Strides, is also a leader in acquisitions in the pharma industry. During his entrepreneurial career spanning more than three decades, he acquired several companies. Those acquisitions are not limited to India but extended to the pharma sector in Australia, Latin America, and Africa.

Arun Kumar never thought of an easy run from the start. He completed his education in Ooty and returned home to join Fathima Matha College, Kollam, for a Bachelor's in Commerce. Arun Kumar attended evening classes and earned for himself engaging in various works during day time. Upon completing the course, at 21, he boarded a train to Mumbai. Aspiration was to find a job in Persia, but hit on an enticing job in Mumbai. So, he parked his dreams of a life in the Middle East aside for a while. His first job was with the Indo-German Alkaloids, Mumbai, for a monthly salary of Rs. 500. Later he worked with Bombay Drug House Private Limited for better remuneration. There he was in charge of export transactions and struck several business deals. It made him confident.

Arun felt that he could earn more if he got export orders for multiple companies independently. He quit his job and, in 1986, began a consultancy firm to spot export markets for pharmaceutical companies. He earned a handsome commission as an agent for several large transactions. Meanwhile, he got married and started living in a small flat in Vashi, Mumbai. His income from consultancy contracts went up. But Arun was sure that it was just the tip of the iceberg. He founded Strides Pharmaceuticals (now known as Strides Pharma Science Limited) in 1990 in a corner of his 600 sq.ft. flat in Mumbai. His earnings from the consultancy business and the money obtained by pawning wife Deepa's gold jewellery were the capital for the venture. Initially, the firm produced generic drugs. Arun, who had a sound understanding of how sales worked, did not have to struggle too long to find the market.

The first export was to Africa. Strides Pharma Science could generate revenue and profit in the first year itself, and the company moved to another building. In 1994, Arun received venture capital funding from Schroders, a global investment firm. The following year he set up a factory in Bengaluru. Infusing more capital matching increased growth was, however, a challenge. Hence several partners were added to help the company grow. K.R. Ravishankar, who owned a company called Caryl Pharma, came onboard. In 1996, Plama Laboratories and ReMed joined hands with Strides.

From the very beginning, Arun Kumar was keen on quality. Emphasis was also laid on transparent transactions. Many giants in the pharma industry came forward to buy Strides' products. Strides won contracts with GlaxoSmithKline Pharmaceuticals Limited (GSK) and Pfizer Inc. Meanwhile, one of its major customers, Arcolab, agreed to invest in Strides, but with a condition - that the name Arcolab be added to Strides. In 1997, the company changed its name to Strides Arcolab. In 1998, a soft gelatin capsule plant was set up in Bengaluru. The following year,

Arun Kumar and his wife Deepa

Strides expanded its presence to the Latin American market by investing in a Brazilian company. In the same year, he acquired a company in Tamil Nadu.

Meanwhile, Strides Arcolab merged with Plama and ReMed. With this, the sales revenue crossed Rs. 100 Crore. Strides' shares were traded on the National Stock Exchange after the merger with Plama, a company listed on the Bombay Stock Exchange, and the headquarters was shifted to Bengaluru. More acquisitions ensured steady growth. The turnover hit Rs.500 Crore, Rs.1,000 Crore, and Rs.1,500 Crore in 2005, 2008 and 2010 respectively. The company's debt increased due to its spending on acquisitions. Arun sold his Australian company at a huge profit and reduced the debt. Three years later, Strides acquired another Australian business and regained its dominance in the Australian market.

Strides, meanwhile, had become a major player in the pharmaceutical and specialty sectors, especially in the field of injectable drugs. About half of the company's revenue came from the injectable specialty division named Agila. In 2013, it was sold to American company Mylan Inc (Now Viatris) for about Rs. 10,000 Crore. It was one of the biggest deals in the Indian pharma industry.

If we ask why pharma is the most profitable business, Arun says it reaps the best value in the market. On Agila divestment, Strides received about ten times its investment. Arun did not forget to let shareholders and employees partake in the party. Strides gave a record dividend in the Indian stock market, Rs. 605 per share (Rs. 500 on 19th December 2013 and Rs. 105 on 16th October 2014). Employees were also given lakhs of rupees in bonuses. Over Rs.4,500 Crore was spent on the two put together.

With Agila's departure, the company's revenue dipped. But Arun reclaimed it within three years with new acquisitions. Chennai-based company Shasun was a major acquisition, and the company changed its name to Strides Shasun Limited. The nine acquisitions made in a year-and-a-half included certain brands of Ranbaxy and Johnson & Johnson.

Arun Kumar in his office

Meanwhile, in 2018, the Active Pharmaceutical ingredients business of Strides was demerged from Strides to form a separate company as Solara Active Pharma Science, a pure-play API business on course to become India's second largest Active Pharmaceutical Ingredient (API) in under four years. Meanwhile, Strides returned to its preferred name as Strides Pharma Science.

Arun also acquired a start-up company called Inbiopro, renamed it Stelis Biopharma, entering the field of biotechnology. The family office of Arun has entered into a strategic partnership with marquee investors to build a global biologics CDMO, specialty injectable and vaccine business with capabilities across several technology platforms. He made entry into the veterinary medicine field and built India's largest fully integrated Animal Health Company - SeQuent Scientific Limited. In less than five years of its major investments, Arun's ownership in SeQuent was divested to the Carlyle Group in a strategic transaction.

Strides currently has eight pharmaceutical factories in India, Africa, United States, Singapore and Europe and a research centre. Its presence extends to 100+ countries with global revenue of Rs. 3,177 crores. The businesses run under Arun's leadership/ownership have a presence in 100+ countries with 7000+ employees with over 30 global manufacturing facilities, with Strides making inspiring strides.

Arun attempted the road less travelled. He entered the difficult injectable drug business and dominated it. When all the pharmaceutical companies headed to the US market, Arun chose Australia and won.

Arun Kumar believes that entrepreneurship is a long journey. There may not be a long-term vision in the beginning. "We will do everything on our own, and those who stand with us have to be sincere. The gate of growth opens gradually. Building a loyal team at this point is a big challenge, and emotions have no place in the path of growth. It is important to trust and let professionals carry out their responsibilities in their way.

Certain steps may go wrong, but make sure not to repeat the mistakes," he says. Arun succeeded on different fronts to make his mark. He carefully maintained discipline from the beginning on all facets, especially money management.

"One enters the entrepreneurship world by giving up everything in one's possession. This journey does not have the security of a job that pays well every month. This journey should aim for absolute success. Entrepreneurship is easy when you are willing to build your way rather than blindly following your predecessors," says Arun.

ARUN KUMAR

Arun Kumar is a first-generation entrepreneur and is known for his intellect of picking 'difficult to operate' domains with high scarcity value. He founded Strides Pharma Science Limited (Strides) in 1990 and has since led the company in building a global reputation with a differentiated business model and delivering value for its stakeholders.

Besides founding Strides, Arun's family office (setup in the early 2000s) run a differentiated set of investments spread across several companies with a combined revenue base over a billion dollars and an invested capital over half a billion dollars. Arun is credited to have co-founded and built India's largest fully integrated Animal Health Company – SeQuent Scientific Limited in less than five years of its major investments. Arun's ownership in SeQuent was divested to the Carlyle Group in May 2020 in a strategic transaction. Arun is the promoter of Solara Active Pharma Sciences, a pure-play API company on course to become India's second largest API business in under four years.

The businesses run under Arun's leadership/ownership have a presence in 100+ countries with 7,000+ employees with over 25 global manufacturing facilities world over.

Arun is a recipient of E&Y Entrepreneur of the Year Award in the Healthcare sector in 2000. He has also been awarded the Business Today 'India Best CEO Award (Mid- Sized Companies Category)' and the 'Best CEO in the Pharma & Healthcare Industry' in 2014.

He was born in 1961 to N.K.K. Pillai and Rajeswari Amma, natives of Kavanadu, Kollam. He and his wife Deepa have two children, Aditya, and Tarini.

15

SCALING DIZZY HEIGHTS

Born into a traditional, middle-class family in Kizhakkambalam town in central Kerala, the interest and proficiency of VK - as he is fondly called by friends - in science saw him earning an Engineering degree in the year 1977. The passion for higher studies was so overpowering that VK took the unlikely step of refusing jobs that came his way. He qualified to enrol for post-graduation in Aeronautical Engineering at the IIT, Kanpur. VK can't precisely recall when he saw an aeroplane for the first time. But it did make a vivid impression on his mind, defining his future journey.

VK started his career as a computer science faculty in the Indian Army. Later, he joined the IT division of Air India, where he played a vital role in the worldwide implementation of the airlines' computerized passenger services systems. Two years later, in 1983, he moved overseas to join the Emirates Group in Dubai, an airline conglomerate that was beginning to show signs of promise in a largely untested region of the world. VK remained with the group for 15 years, formulating and implementing Information Technology strategies for its global operations and contributing significantly to the airline's growth into what it is today. At the time of leaving, VK held the post of General Manager-IT of the Emirates Group, hitting a glass ceiling for Indian expatriates.

Over a decade and a half in the aviation industry brought insights and a deep understanding of the business, the systems, the processes, and the pain points. VK realized a lot more could be done to change the way people travelled. But working within the confines of a system laid out by others was hardly the right recipe for his ideas to take wings. To create transformational solutions, he needed to work unfettered. That was how the spirit of entrepreneurship was kindled. However, leaving a high-profile job and a steady income to start a venture was no easy decision. And coming from a society rooted in tradition than in daring, did not help matters. But not surprisingly, VK followed his heart and took the plunge. IBS was established in 1997 with 55 inexperienced engineering graduates.

The '90s saw IT services being outsourced to India in a big way. The cost arbitrage of Indian IT talent offered great business opportunities in back-office operations, systems integration, maintenance, and support. More and more entrepreneurs began tapping into this potential, leading to the mushrooming of IT services companies in India. But the 'services' model was not what VK had in mind. To bring about a transformation that would touch the lives of millions, an IT services venture was not an option. IP creation and value addition were what VK intended to bring to the table. IBS had to go to the unchartered territory of being a product-driven technology company.

The choice of location was unconventional too. In the '90s, Bangalore was the natural choice for IT startups. VK defied all portents, challenged existing paradigms, and went ahead to start operations in what was perceived to be the most industry hostile region in India - Kerala. The love for the home state was overwhelming. Looking back, VK says, "investing and staying invested in Kerala is one of the most fulfilling business decisions of my life."

As with any entrepreneurial venture, the initial days were a mix of circus, nervousness, trepidation, and hope. Investing the entire life savings to start an IT product company was fraught with risks. A major chunk of the spending had to be channelled into building technology products that offered no guarantee of taking off. Domain experience or expertise was not available locally either. Brick by brick, VK built capacity, influenced thoughts, attitude, and behaviour, and gave leadership to a set of young people.

V.K.Mathews receiving KMA Management Leadership Award -2013 from Oommen Chandy, the then Chief Minister of Kerala

Today VK continues to head IBS Software as its Executive Chairman, scripting one of the most enduring success stories coming out of India in the IT product landscape. Unlike the services companies that make up an overwhelming majority of the Indian IT landscape, an IT product SaaS company like IBS Software is at the higher end of the value chain. IBS remains the architects, designers, and builders of technology products that typically address the needs of the industry 10-20 years ahead.

IBS Software's products control mission-critical operations where even a brief disruption of work could mean not only losing millions of dollars in downtime but also jeopardizing the safety of people. In the aviation sector, IBS Software provides end-to-end IT systems across all process areas – airline passenger services, cargo operations, flight and crew operations, airport operations, and aircraft maintenance engineering. In fact, no other single enterprise in the world offers this range of IT products to the aviation industry.

Today, IBS Software's technology solutions are used by 10 of the 20 largest airlines/airline groups globally, 4 of the 5 largest global oil companies, and over 80 of the largest hotel chains and 30 travel suppliers in the world. Nearly 70% of the air cargo movement in and out of Japan and Australia is powered by IBS Software. As it enters its 25th year in 2021, IBS Software serves over 200 clients worldwide, employing 3500 professionals from 20 nationalities.

V.K.Mathews and his wife Latha

During its journey, IBS Software has acquired seven international companies (in Europe, USA, Canada and India), significantly enhancing its portfolio of software offerings and ramping up its managerial bandwidth.

In 2015, making one of the biggest investments in an Indian IT product company, Blackstone, the world's largest private equity player, became a minority shareholder of IBS Software. Today, IBS Software is Kerala's largest unicorn with a valuation of around $1.50 billion (Credit Suisse 2021 report).

What sets V.K. Mathews apart is his high degree of emotional intelligence - self-awareness, self-regulation, empathy, and social skill. Values, the defining characteristic of his leadership, have built the reputation and credibility of IBS Software. These values serve as benchmarks for employees to make independent decisions as they go about their daily duties. As a result, the finest principles of propriety are hardcoded in the collective psyche of IBSians.

Truly one of the most inspiring business stories to come out of Kerala.

V.K. MATHEWS

A visionary entrepreneur who combined business instincts and innovation with corporate ethics and societal expectations, V.K. Mathews established IBS Software, one of the most accomplished software product companies globally at Thiruvananthapuram Technopark, in 1997. V.K.Mathews was born in Kizhakkambalam, Ernakulam, to K.P.Korath, the founder manager of Federal Bank and Kunjamma.

Apart from a Master's degree in Aeronautical Engineering from IIT, Kanpur, V.K. Mathews has had executive management education from Harvard Business School, Boston, USA. Over the years, V.K. Mathews has emerged as a thought leader in the global aviation industry and is a regular speaker at various international events and seminars. He was the Executive Council member of NASSCOM, past Chairman of CII Kerala, and is currently a Member of CII Southern Regional Council.

He has received several awards from the Government, media, and trade associations. He currently resides in Dubai with his wife, Latha. The couple have two daughters, Hannah and Maria.

16

GEO + JIT MAKES GEOJIT

Never in his wildest dreams did C.J.George think that he would make his name as a businessman as his family has an agrarian background and to add to it, he was a Left-leaning youth. After completing his M.Com. from Kerala University, he went to Delhi with the dream of becoming a lawyer. Soon after, he got a job as an equity research analyst at Batlivala and Karani, a top stock broking company, which has always been an area of interest to him. George delved into the world of securities for a monthly stipend of Rs.750, while in the evenings he was busy with his LLB course. The rich experience George gained, and the lessons learned at the firm were priceless. Six months later, he was transferred to the firm's Kochi branch office at double the stipend and George's LLB dream came to an end.

The capital market scene in the 80s was opaque, less regulated and open to malpractice by unscrupulous brokers and sub-brokers. Most of the brokers were proprietary traders who also indulged in broking at times! Genuine investors found it difficult to participate in the capital market. George had experienced all these first-hand and was truly moved by the plight of the investors.

George's job as a financial analyst and stock dealer prompted him to apply for a Ph.D. to research the topic 'Valuation of Stocks'. It was a tough job balancing work as well as his studies, so George decided to leave the job and fully concentrate on completing his Ph.D.

Former President of India A.P.J.Abdul Kalam at the 23rd anniversary
celebration of Geojit. C.J.George is behind him

Coincidence or fate, at the same time, his friend and client, Ranajit Kanjilal, impressed by George's keen interest in stock market suggested they set up a brokerage together. In a short span of six weeks, George's life took a new turn, he became a member of Cochin Stock Exchange and founded Messrs C.J. George and Co. He set up the office in a garage converted beside Ranajit's house, but Ranajit was unable to become a partner of the venture as only Stock Exchange members could be partners in a stock broking firm as per the rules.

Several clients from Baltivala and Karani joined George's new venture. Even though 1987 was not a good year for the stock market, George's new company managed to reap profits in its first year. Within a short time, his company became one of the leading stock broking firms in Kochi. In 1988, Ranajit, on gaining membership in Cochin Stock Exchange, become a partner of the firm. At the suggestion of Ranajit's wife, they combined their names, GEO from George and JIT from Ranajit, and thus was born 'Geojit', a new company with an office in Kochi.

George informed his family about his new business venture only after 18 months of setting it up. The company was profitable right from the first month, so it was a pleasant surprise for all. But with the Harshad Mehta scam in 1992, the stock market took a toll and Geojit was also was affected, leading to Ranajit's exit from the partnership in 1993, once again making the company a sole proprietorship. George established two Geojit branches in Thrissur and Muvattupuzha during this difficult time. He always believed that investment in expansion is always better during difficult times as every penny will be spent well!

The Harshad Mehta scam paved the way for greater transparency and controls in the stock market. During this time, the National Stock Exchange (NSE) came into being, but the membership cost crores of rupees. Geojit became a private company in 1994 and needed more capital to further develop and expand the company. George approached the Kerala State Industrial Development Corporation Ltd. (KSIDC), and after due diligence, KSIDC acquired a 24 percent stake in the company investing Rs.50 lakh.

On Geojit becoming a corporate broking house, George expanded his business outside of Kerala, establishing branches in Coimbatore and Mumbai in 1994. The following year, Geojit became a member of the NSE. Geojit became one of the first companies outside of Mumbai to provide online trading facilities for NSE. The same year, Geojit made an Initial Public Offering (IPO) and got listed on the Bombay Stock Exchange, becoming the first stock broking company to do so.

While other stock broking companies grew via sub-broking firms, Geojit thrived on the franchisee basis, cutting a new path. By being one of the earliest depository participants in the country of National Securities Depository Limited (NSDL) in 1996, Geojit provided pioneering service of Demating share certificates electronically. Two years later, Geojit became a member of the Bombay Stock Exchange too. At that time Geojit became the one with highest number of VSAT terminals in the country to connect branches with NSE for online trading. Geojit not only took pioneering steps to convert physical share certificates to electronic entries in the country, the company also saw to it that the home state

Kerala become the first Indian state where at least one demat account is opened in every Pin Code in the state.

C.J.George and his wife Shiny with their sons Jones and Jyotis and daughters-in-law Annie and Ann

Geojit, a company from the South Indian State of Kerala, made its way to becoming a leading Indian retail stock broking company at a time when stock brokers from Maharashtra, Gujarat, and Bengal dominated the Indian stock market. To cater to the needs of Non-Resident Indians, George planned to establish business outside India and, in 2001, partnered with Barjeel under the Al-Saud Group in UAE to form Barjeel Geojit. By 2011, Geojit had spread across Kingdom of Saudi Arabia, Kuwait, Bahrain, and Oman. The Bank of Bahrain and Kuwait too became a partner. Geojit grew to be a complete financial services company, offering mutual funds and insurance apart from broking. Geojit started a Non-Banking Financial Company under the name, Geojit Credits in 2005 for lending against securities as collateral which was not developed.

With the help of advanced technology, Geojit was able to pioneer in the stock broking business. In 2000, Geojit became the first stock broking company in India to allow investors to trade through internet at the comfort of investor's choice of location, and in 2010, introduced mobile trading in India. Geojit Technologies, a sister concern, aimed to develop state-of-the-art technologies for the financial services field was started in 2003. In 2004, Rakesh Jhunjhunwala, the renowned Indian equity investor, took a significant stake in the company and continues to hold the stake even in 2021.

In 2006, the French banking group BNP Paribas took a 33 percent stake in the company, creating history in the Indian stock broking field. From being one out of the 9,000 stock broking companies in 1987, Geojit today has over 460 branches in different parts of the country and the Middle East. The company employs around 2500 people. Geojit handles the investments of over 10 lakh investors and as on 30th June 2021, the company's Assets Under Custody and Management stood at Rs. 56,000 crores.

Geojit could reap rich profits for its shareholders. If one had invested Rs.1,000 in its shares in 1995, its value is now Rs. 3.21 lakh*. Moreover, such investors would have already received Rs. 71,745 as dividend on such shares. The KSIDC invested Rs. 50 lakhs in 1994-95 and they have already received dividend of Rs. 35.87 crores on their shares. Shares worth Rs. 50 lakh then have a value of Rs.160.60 crore* today.

The efforts by C.J.George have made a monumental impact on the stock broking industry in the country as well as for investors. Geojit took pioneering private efforts to educate investors to create long term wealth which had a role in the burgeoning investor population in the state of Kerala, particularly and in southern states. The Economic Times listed Geojit as one of the top ten brands of the first decade of this millennium along with marquee brands such as Infosys, Bollywood etc. His company strives for transparency with its purpose of existence being to create wealth for its clients. The biggest life lesson he wishes to pass on after three-decades in the stock market is this: "There are no shortcuts in life; only hard work can yield success."

* Closing Market price as on October 08, 2021 – Rs. 80.30

C.J. GEORGE

Does the name Geojit ring a bell? Welcome to the world of C.J. George, founder and Managing Director of one of India's leading investment services companies, Geojit Financial Services Ltd. He is at present the Managing Committee Member of the Associated Chambers of Commerce & Industry of India (ASSOCHAM), New Delhi, the Advisory Committee Member of Indian Clearing Corporation Limited (ICCL) and a member of the syndicate of Cochin University of Science and Technology (CUSAT).

His directorships other than in Geojit group companies include, Kerala State Industrial Development Corporation Limited (KSIDC), Kerala Infrastructure Fund Management Ltd, V-Guard Industries Ltd and Aster DM Healthcare Ltd. He was the executive committee member of the National Stock Exchange of India (NSE) and National Securities Depository Ltd (NSDL). He is the recipient of several awards, including the KMA Management Leadership Award.

C.J.George was born in Paingottoor, Ernakulam, in 1959 to Matthew John and Annamma. His wife Shiny, was Head of the Statistics Department at Mar Athanasius College, Kothamangalam. The couple has two sons, Jones and Jyotis. Jones is married to Annie and Jyotis to Ann.

17

FAIZAL FORWARD

P.K. Ahmmed the owner of Peekay Group, Kozhikode always believed that education was the most valuable asset he could give to his children. This conviction contributed to Faizal attending the best educational institutions and helped him step out of his comfort zone by attending college outside of Kerala, at the Manipal Institute of Technology, where he earned his bachelor's degree in Civil Engineering. This experience inculcated a sense of adventure and a passion for exploration that endures even today. Faizal went on to graduate with an MBA in Business Administration & Operations from the T.A.Pai Management Institute. Continuing his pursuit of education, Faizal obtained a Master's degree in Industrial Engineering from Bradley University in the USA, while also juggling a part-time job as a delivery boy for Domino's Pizza and maintaining his scholarship. He continued to gain footing professionally as he joined the Inductotherm Group in New Jersey where he gained experience as an industrial engineer.

Upon returning to India, Faizal was entrusted with the Kottikollon family-run factory, Peekay Steels in Kozhikode. This was the start of his entrepreneurial journey and what drove him to seek avenues for innovation in various markets. In the summer of 1995, Faizal visited Dubai and correctly identified it as a land filled with potential. Despite his family's doubts, his conviction in the city helped bolster his excitement and commitment at the opportunity.

As Faizal explored the city he found that the cost of imported steel, especially from America, was far less in Dubai than it was in India. He saw this as a cost-effective way to supply high quality products to India and began to establish his business, with his father as his first customer. As his client base grew, he established Al Ahmadi General Trading for dealing and trading steel in Ajman.

He acutely observed that Dubai had the resources to produce steel and other raw materials domestically and by tapping into this opportunity, Faizal was able to make huge advancements in the Middle Eastern steel foundry and valve industry. Faizal and Shabana established Emirates Techno Casting (ETC) and rapidly scaled up the company through sheer resourcefulness. Faizal noticed that valves needed in refineries were not manufactured in the Middle East, but instead, imported from Europe and America. By manufacturing these valves in the Middle East, ETC helped cut down transportation times from three months to a mere twenty days. Demand for these valves boomed and orders started pouring in as companies began to rely on ETC for their valves. Price hikes for petroleum products further bolstered business and the company expanded to set up two more steel plants. By 2007, the company started producing the valves themselves. Middle East oil companies were eager to work with Faizal and businesses like Saudi Aramco, Qatar Petroleum, Abu Dhabi National Oil Company, Kuwait Petroleum, and others started buying valves from Faizal. It was the first foundry in the UAE to implement manufacturing integration and was one of only two foundries in the world to have a Vacuum Oxygen Argon Degassing Furnace. This immense growth led to ETC being branded as one of the top three most technologically advanced foundries in the world.

In 2007, Faizal and Shabana took their company to the Arab Oil and Gas Exhibition. ETC was featured in an article that generated a lot of interest and soon after, Dubai Holding – a global investment holding company owned by H.H. Sheikh Mohammed Bin Rashid Al Maktoum – bought shares in ETC. By the next year, Dubai Holding owned 45% of the company's shares at a valuation of $300 million. Even as Dubai's market fluctuated, ETC remained stable and Faizal successfully sold his flagship venture for $400 million to TYCO International. During this time, Faizal and Shabana not only built their business but also gained a reputation as advocates for a healthy and well balanced lifestyle. At ETC, they opened The Faizal and Shabana Community Center, a place where employees could exercise and relax. Incorporating this sense of wellness at their office space contributed heavily to employee satisfaction and loyalty.

Faizal Kottikollon and his wife, Shabana Faizal, with their children,
Sophiya, Sarah, Zachariah and Czarina

Faizal's pursuit of unique experiences led him to Europe where he connected with companies and individuals at every level. It was here that he learnt about the prefabricated construction method that had emerged in Sweden and Denmark. This avant-garde building method used robotic technology to produce specific structures in factories that could then be assembled on site. This meant that hospitals, hotels, schools and homes could be built in a fraction of the time, something that would be invaluable in growing economies like India and in the Middle East.

Not content to just learn about these methods, Faizal and Shabana wanted to share their success and use it to provide opportunities to disadvantaged children. To understand how they could best do so, they visited the Government Vocational Higher Secondary School for Girls (GVHSS) at Nadakkavu in Kozhikode and found that re-designing schools to maximise the benefits of education could greatly help certain areas. To get material that met their standards, the pair opened KEF Infra 1, the world's biggest offset prefabricated manufacturing factory. Projects such as the Infosys campus, GEMS Modern Academy in Kochi, the Indira Canteens in Karnataka and Embassy 7B in Bangalore were all products of this factory. They also transformed the school in Nadakkavu with the help of KEF Infra 1 to become a world-class institution. It has been ranked among top three in Education World India School Rankings 2020-21, and is now a flag-bearer of excellence in education in India because of its focus on holistic development. Now the Nadakkavu model has already replicated into 141 government schools in Kerala and has impacted 300000 students positively. Keral government has decided to replicate Nadakkavu model to 1000 schools which will have an positive impact for more that 1 million students.

Faizal had taken over the worlds of manufacturing and infrastructure but through it all has focused on health and wellness.

He is a practicing yogi and has been a fitness enthusiast for over 25 years. Faizal and Shabana were the very first residents, who donated 10 million dirhams to Al Jalila Foundation, which is a global philanthropic organisation dedicated to transforming lives through medical education and research. The grant is being used for cutting-edge research in cancer, cardiovascular, diabetes, obesity and mental health.

Faizal Kottikollon with Ratan Tata, Chairman Emeritus of Tata Sons

With a goal of making premium quality healthcare accessible to all, Faizal and Shabana also established Meitra Hospital in Kozhikode. Meitra is a 450,000-square-foot, 220-bed, quaternary-care hospital and was manufactured in just 18 months, using KEF Infra's offsite manufacturing technology. In 2021, Meitra rolled out the next phase of the hospital bringing patients, doctors as well as primary, secondary, tertiary and critical care service providers under one integrated system, connected through hard and soft infrastructure. This is the next step towards making healthcare accessible to all for a fraction of the cost. Faizal believes that equal opportunity must be provided to everyone, the opportunity to prevent illness through wellness. Faizal's dream project emerged from this thought. Tulah Wellness Resort, India's first unique integrated wellness resort at Chelambra, near Calicut International Airport, in Kerala. A self-sufficient resort that produces and utilizes its own green electricity, water, organic food and waste is being built using manufacturing automation and BIM systems, reducing cost and time. Tulah Resort aims to be a one stop shop for any and all traditional practices as well as modern technology to help support you in your wellness journey.

As their flourishing businesses grow, Faizal and Shabana are always looking for ways to give back to society. One of the goals of the Faizal and Shabana Foundation is to initiate positive change. As a team, they often travel to their homeland looking for every chance to bring about an impact that insights the creation of an equitable future for everyone. To date, the foundation has supported and empowered more than 25 community initiatives, donated in excess of $20 million and impacted hundreds of thousands of lives. As a result, they have created a ripple effect that has impacted the lives of thousands of people across India and the UAE.

This persistent curiosity to insight change and bring about better lives for as many people is one of the marks of a true leader. Someone who looks after the economic, social, physical and mental health of individuals. Faizal and Shabana have changed the lives of so many while maintaining their humility, kindness and integrity throughout the process. Every big project has been preceded by a humble thought, a solution for a problem faced by many. That is the essence of the KEF empire, finding innovative ways to solve modern problems.

FAIZAL E. KOTTIKOLLON

In the most unassuming of places is where the best entrepreneurs build businesses. And one such person, who consistently refuses to be bound by the limits of what they can achieve, is Faizal E. Kottikollon. Faizal is the Founder and Chairman of KEF Holdings, Chairman of the Board at Meitra Hospital and Co-Founder/Vice Chairperson of The Faizal & Shabana Foundation. He has also established Tulah, a unique integrated wellness resort at Chelambra, near Calicut International Airport, in Kerala.

Born in 1963 to P.K. Ahmmed and Safiya, Faizal has always valued strong family bonds. Faizal and his wife, Shabana Faizal, have carried forward this ethos as they parent four children, Sophiya, Sarah, Zachariah and Czarina, to build a cohesive and loving family.

18
WHAT DREAMS ARE MADE OF

Born to Dominic Joseph of the Pala Kuruvinakkunnel family in 1950, Jose Dominic's childhood witnessed the mass migration of Keralites to the Gulf region, and he longed to visit the US and the Gulf. After completing his Bachelor's in Commerce from Loyola College, Chennai, he joined the Chartered Accountancy course in 1971. He joined the Bangalore-based Brahmayya and Co. as an articled clerk or trainee solicitor. In 1975, he became a fully qualified CA and started a new job at AF Ferguson and Co. in Mumbai. By now, most of his peers had left for the US, and his childhood dreams of a life in the Gulf and the US got reignited. But he married Anita from Thiruvananthapuram and settled down in Mumbai to start his family life. Soon, Jose Dominic received a letter from his father informing him of his deteriorating health. His father told him that he needed Jose's help back home to look after the family hotel. Jose's dreams of going abroad lay shattered, while he was also unsure of handling the family business. Despite his father's repeated calls, Jose could not make up his mind. He wrote a resignation letter but could not hand it over to his boss for a month. All Jose wanted to do was leave India to chase his dreams, but that seemed impossible in the new circumstance. Finally, after mulling over his predicament for a month, he made up his mind; he would go back and assist his father for two years, but after that, he would hand over everything to his brothers. In 1978, putting a lock on his aspirations, he left his job and returned home.

THE LEGACY OF A FATHER

Dominic Joseph owned the hotel 'Casino' on Willingdon Island in Kochi. Though it was started as a modest restaurant in 1957, Casino later emerged as a vast 32-room hotel. In 1954, Dominic Joseph kicked off his hotel business by hiring the lease rights of the Malabar Hotel (currently Taj Malabar), which was owned by the Cochin Port Trust. To protect his workers after the termination of the agreement, he launched Hotel Casino. Initially, he partnered with notable shipping industrialists Achuthan Pillai, D.B.Khona, and W.H. D'Cruz. D'Cruz, who had just come back from a European trip, suggested the name Casino. But the restaurant was not getting the profit they wanted, so they also built hotel rooms. Dominic's partners soon shed their shares, but hotel rooms became sought-after as shipping companies, exporting firms, and tea businesses on the island began to grow in number. Jose came home to witness this bustling scenario.

Jose Dominic and his wife Anita

The Indian Hotel Company, owners of the Taj Hotel network, come under the Tata Group. Luckily its Managing Director, A.B.Kerkar, was

Jose's former client in Mumbai. Clueless about the hotel business, he conferred with Kerkar, who turned out to be a metaphorical investment in his entrepreneurial career. Kerkar advised him that a hotel can succeed only by being a part of a conglomerate or a sub-set of a prolific business. Keeping this suggestion in mind, Jose increased the number of rooms of Casino to 68 and accelerated income.

Meanwhile, in 1987, Prime Minister Rajiv Gandhi visited Lakshadweep and presented the idea of developing Bangaram Island into a tourism hub. Later, the central tourism minister sent letters to hotel owners inviting them to start resorts on the island. The government transported the bidders in a helicopter, and Jose Dominic joined the team only to experience the trip and Bangaram. He was surprised to meet the representatives of hotel giants. After a day's stay at the government guest house in Bangaram, they moved to Agatti. Lakshadweep administrator Vajjahat Habibullah asked the hotel owners about their tourism plans in Bangaram. Representatives of most hotel giants sought more time to study business possibilities and come up with an investment of Rs.50-60 crores. When it was Jose Dominic's turn to speak, he said that he did not need more time to decide and that he planned to construct a resort within three months. The resorts would be modelled on the houses of the natives, and the cottages will have palm roofs, all environment-friendly.

To everyone's amazement, Jose Dominic bagged the contract in October 1988. The resort was supposed to be opened before the inauguration of the Agatti airport in December. He had a 30-room guest house and 15 acres of land for 25 years on lease on Bangaram Island. The government set the condition that no natural resource on the island should be used to build the resorts. Close to 100 workers landed from Kochi, and even the sand for construction works was shipped from outside. With that, Jose expanded beyond Hotel Casino. Initially, 15 rooms were made at the 'Bangaram Island Resort.' All passengers of Vayudoot, the first flight to land at the Agatti Airport, were accommodated at the resort.

Jose Dominic receiving Athithya Ratna Award

While TV, A/C, swimming pools, a multi-cuisine restaurant, and room service were marketed as the attractive features of other resorts, the main allure of Bangaram Island Resort was the pristine beauty of nature. Foreign travellers came to Lakshadweep after staying in luxurious hotels in Mumbai, so the rent for a room per night was fixed at $180, which was on par with the rates of five-star hotels in the metropolis. Travel agents were shocked to hear this. They did not understand the allure of the new palm leaf and clay resort. They requested Jose to reduce the rent to attract tourists, but Jose could not be reasoned with.

A VISION UNFOLDING

The Bangaram Island Resort changed the definition of luxury hotels. By conserving nature and providing job opportunities for natives, the resort made an excellent dwelling for travellers with its aura amid the pristine beauty of nature. The government took significant measures to bring in tourists. Foreign journalists came to Lakshadweep, and they wrote about the resort. Wealthy travellers soon started flocking to the resort. The success of Bangaram Island Resort raised Jose Dominic's confidence, giving his dreams a new direction.

Starting the resort turned out to be a great learning experience for Jose Dominic. He started another resort called 'Spice Village' in Thekkady in 1991. Spice Village was also developed without any modern amenities like TV or A/C, and only ethnic food varieties were included in the menu. That was the first private hotel in Kerala built outside a major city. The room rates were on the higher side here as well, yet the new venture turned out to be a great success within a short period.

Finally, Jose had found his calling, and now there was no stopping him. Within two years, he opened a lake resort named 'Coconut Lagoon' in Kumarakom, the first of its kind in the state. With the economy taking off on the strength of expatriate remittances, many people preferred to demolish their old, traditional houses and build concrete houses instead. Jose saw an opportunity here. He purchased the roofs, cabins, and other materials of such demolished houses and used them to build Coconut Lagoon in the traditional way. Always on the lookout to expand the family business, Jose came to know that his friend Babu Varghese had launched the first houseboat of Kerala in Alappuzha. Jose requested Babu to build one for him as well, and thus he became the owner of the second houseboat in the state.

However, the tourism sector faced a major setback in 1994 due to the plague outbreak in Surat, Gujarat. Foreign travellers stopped coming in, but Indian travellers kept trickling in. Coconut Lagoon became the honeymoon destination for Gujarati couples. Soon Jose established resorts named 'Marari Beach' in Mararikulam and 'Brunton Boatyard' in Kochi in 1996 and 1998 respectively. There was a spurt in arrivals again with the Kerala Government promoting tourism with the tagline 'God's Own Country.'

By now, Jose Dominic had his signature style - every resort was constructed with low investment while keeping the tradition of Kerala and the beauty of nature intact. It ensured high profits. The Casino Group of Hotels was renamed CGH Earth in 2004. Kollengode Palace of Palakkad was taken over and renovated to build an Ayurveda resort named 'Kalari Kovilakam' in the same year. Later, Swaswara, a yoga-based resort in Gokarna, Karnataka, and Vanavasa, a rural attraction, were also set up. There is no significant place in Kerala that Jose's entrepreneurial eyes have missed. He launched the 'Wayanad Wild' resort in Vythiri and converted Chittoor Palace into an ultra-premium resort. He has forayed into Tamil Nadu and Puducherry as well.

CGH Earth has 20 resorts spread out all over Kerala, Tamil Nadu, Puducherry, and Karnataka. CGH Earth is among the enterprises of the Dominic brothers. In 2018, Jose Dominic retired as the head of the group but continues to be on the board of directors. The group has a company, CAFS, providing food services at airports, on flights, highways, and railway stations. Another commendable initiative by Jose is JGT Living Space, a real estate company.

Jose has not only inspired the aspiring entrepreneurs but his family as well. His wife Anita currently runs an organic farm and homestay in Pala. His children Mridula, George Joseph, and Dominic K. Joseph, are all associated with CGH Earth, carrying forward their grandfather and father's legacies.

Jose Dominic is a unique entrepreneur who revealed that beyond grand buildings, there's a luxury. He believed that sustainable living has many benefits and successfully implemented innovative ideas. Jose didn't go for compromises. After a 30-year entrepreneurial life, he feels that absolute success can be attained only by holding onto values. CGH Earth took its own path to maintain those values and achieved eminence and prosperity.

JOSE DOMINIC

People who have earned a place for themselves through toil and unwavering resolve make it a point to lead by example. They do not impose their ideas but inspire. Such an entrepreneur values failures as much as he seeks success but does not accept defeat.

Jose Dominic is one such entrepreneur who has inspired thousands of people in his line of work. He was the CEO and Managing Director of the premier South Indian hotel network, CGH Earth. An enduring presence in the trade spectrum, Jose Dominic was the founding president of Kerala Travel Mart (KTM). He functioned as the chairman and president of Confederation of Indian Industry (CII), Kerala chapter, and TiE Kerala, respectively. He also served on the advisory panel of the central and state tourism departments. He was conferred with numerous awards by the central and state tourism departments for his feats in the tourism sector. Jose Dominic was also bestowed the Management Leadership Award by the Kerala Management Association, Best Entrepreneurship Award by the TiE Kerala, Green Globe Award by World Travel Mart, and the Pacific Asia Travel Associations Award.

19

WALKING AHEAD OF
THE TIMES

O/E/N India was founded in 1968 by Pamela's father Mathew. In 1973, she took charge as the Executive Officer of the company. For the next 13 years, the father-daughter duo worked side by side to keep the company moving.

Before O/E/N India came into being, Mathew worked for long with the refrigeration technology company Voltas, of the Tata group. Since the company did not see higher professional prospects in Kerala he was moved to Mumbai. However, Mathew, who had a rural background, could not adapt to the fast-paced life in Mumbai. He quit the job, returned to his hometown, and joined as project development manager at Travancore Rayons at Perumbavoor. When he realized that the job did not offer him any worthwhile prospects he thought about his own venture.

With a good network in the industry, it did not take long for Mathew to strike a deal with the US manufacturer Oak Electro Netics (later OAK Industries Inc). He started a distribution agency in India for OAK's products Relays & Switches and represented a German Company Hartings for sale of connectors in India. He soon collaborated with the US Company OAK to independently create a manufacturing unit under the brand O/E/N India. The new company, incorporated in 1968, commenced production in 1969 at its first plant in Mulanthuruthy, Ernakulam. 45 percent of O/E/N

India shares were owned by its US collaborator and 25 percent ownership was bought by the Kerala State Industrial Development Corporation (KSIDC). Mathew, his family & friends owned the remaining 30 percent stake.

At the outset, the components manufactured were supplied mainly to the Defence. As years lapsed, electronic components needed for other applications were also developed. Therefore, in 1973, O/E/N India established its own Research and Development (R&D) wing followed by setting up own Tool Room in 1974 to build tools for O/E/N products. The company expanded to unchartered territories of Telecommunication and Automobile — waters that only a handful of people in the country dared to test then. Nearly 50 years later, product supply to Defence is only about 5 percent of the total production, while the automobile sector is in the range of 50-60 percent and rest for various Industrial applications.

Pamela Anna Mathew receiving Confederation of Indian Industry (CII) Award from Ratan Tata, the then Chairman of Tata Group

At present, O/E/N India supplies to Automobile companies like Maruti Suzuki, Tata Motors, Mahindra and Mahindra, Renault, Honda, and Ford in the four wheeler segment; TVS/Bajaj/Royal Enfield in the two wheeler segment. O/E/N India has always been a key driving force in the growth of the country's automobile industry. Everything was made possible by O/E/N India's factory located at Electrogiri in Mulanthuruthy, a small town just 15 km away from Kochi, supported by its R&D and Captive Tool Room.

In 1986, after the demise of Mathew, Pamela's mother Sarah Mathew took over as the Managing Director of the company while Pamela Anna Mathew became its Executive Director. Later, she became the Joint Managing Director, then Managing Director and presently Chairman & Managing Director.

In a span of three decades, Pamela helped the company prosper enviably. Today, she is targeting an annual growth of 20% to 25%. To achieve this goal, the company has set up two advanced factories in Pune apart from the Bangalore and the Special Economic Zone, Kochi, factories.

After the long term experience since 1966 representing the German connector manufacturer, O/E/N wanted to start manufacture connectors also. The decision to produce connectors prompted O/E/N India to associate with Souriau, a French Company as the German Company with whom they had association was not ready in early 1980 to start manufacturing in India. The foreign investment policy of the time did not allow a second foreign investor for O/E/N India apart from the US-based Oak Industries, owning a significant share in the company.

Hence, a new company named O/E/N Connectors was formed. Both O/E/N India and KSIDC owned stakes in this new entity without equity participation from Souriau. Soon after launch in 1981, it forayed to the stock market with an IPO. Souriau, which provided only technical assistance initially, invested in equity (26%)in the company in 1989. Later, Souriau was sold to Framatome Connectors International (FCI). As of now Amphenol owns the company, hence no longer part of O/E/N India. During early 1980s, the O/E/N Group also founded O/E/N Microsystem, which manufactured computer peripherals like keyboards, display terminals, and floppy discs. The company was later merged with the Parent company as the products manufactured were discontinued.

Over the years, one of the biggest challenges before Pamela was to buy back the shares owned by OAK in O/E/N India. She was successful in buying back 45 percent of the shares by the mid-1990s. Today 51 percent of O/E/N India's shares belong to Pamela and her family, while KSIDC retains 25 percent.

Pamela's funda? A smile spreads positively on her face, even in the most intensely stressful situations. She believes that the pieces of advice given by her father have been an asset in her journey.

Pamela Anna Mathew receiving KSIDC's Entrepreneur Award from Oommen Chandy, the then Chief Minister of Kerala

TRADITIONAL VALUES

K.A. Mathew was in the habit of personally wishing employees on their birthdays. Once Pamela joined the company, he entrusted the task to her. Pamela was puzzled first and asked her father why she had to do it; his answer was a cheeky grin. However, soon she could find out the reason. In a large company, this practice helped her know the employees personally. She could address the employees by their names in a crowd, which most people found as a form of recognition. It created in them a sense of belonging to the company.

Pamela is also proud of completing her education in Kerala. Her entrepreneurial experiences have helped shape her life as a wholesome individual. She could build a professional team that can run the company smoothly even in her absence. O/E/N India could create an excellent corporate culture within five decades of its existence. It is the foundation on which the company has gone to achieve steady development and growth.

When Mathew died in 1986, the turnover of the company was Rs.5 crores. Under Pamela – perhaps one of the first women entrepreneurs in the core electronic components manufacturing industry – the company witnessed a splendid 25-fold growth in the next three decades. O/E/N India and its employees could see Pamela carrying forward her father's legacy by basing her goals on kindness, optimism, hard work, and a sense of fellowship. Pamela made sure that the entrepreneurial grit which she inherited from her father cut new paths for her.

PAMELA ANNA MATHEW

Entrepreneurial grit is a rare gift that comes to people who can foresee market possibilities like no other - Pamela Anna Mathew's journey attests to the statement. Pamela was born to K.A. Mathew and Sarah Mathew. She finished her Pre-Degree from UC College, Aluva; completed Bachelor's Degree in Economics from St. Teresa's College, Ernakulam and Master Degree in Economics from Maharajas College Ernakulam. Later, Pamela took an MBA from the Cochin University of Science and Technology (CUSAT).

Pamela Anna Mathew joined her father K.A. Mathew in his entrepreneurial journey in 1973, almost five years after he set up O/E/N India. She is presently its Chairman & Managing Director. She is the first woman to serve as the President of several Industry associations like Cochin Chamber of Commerce, Kerala Management Association and Electronic Component Industries Association. Pamela also chaired the Kerala chapter of the Confederation of Indian Industry (CII). She also serves as a Trustee and Board Member of various educational institutions.

Pamela has received numerous awards, such as the Kerala Management Association's Management Leadership Award in 2011 and the Kerala State Industrial Development Corporation (KSIDC) Entrepreneur Award in 2011. She was adjudged the Best Chairperson at National Level of CII in 2002-03 and received the award from Ratan Tata, the Chairman of the Tata group. Received Lifetime Achievement Award from TIE Kerala in 2019.

Pamela is married to George Varghese. They have a daughter, Roopa, a Mechanical Engineer and a qualified Management Accountant who worked with Glaxo Smith Klein (GSK) initially. Now she is the Executive Director of O/E/N India Ltd.

20

FLAVOURS THAT LINGER

M.E. Meeran introduced packaged flavours that tickle the Malayali palette to homes around the world. His business journey began at Adimali to where he relocated from Kothamangalam in 1964 to start a grocery business. Situated on the Eastern hills, he named his establishment Eastern Trading Company, and it gradually flourished into a significant business entity. By 1976, he had begun wholesale distribution of various products as well.

Meeran embraced the world of flavours by chance. One day, he brought a branded curry powder home from his store along with other groceries to reduce the work burden on his wife. But it drew sharp disapproval from wife Nabeesa, who went hammer and tongs over the quality and taste of the curry powder. She said it was no substitute for her homemade curry powder. The young Meeran thought, "why can't I come out with my curry powder when I have an expert at home?" That marked the beginning of Eastern curry powder.

Readymade curry powder was not popular in Kerala's households then. And it didn't take much time for Meeran's product to conquer kitchens in the state. Today Eastern is a go-to brand that delivers a truly Malayali culinary experience.

Meeran's father Ibrahim had owned a grocery shop in Nellimattom. He was already following one of the oldest lessons in running a business: the customer is king. His customers trusted Ibrahim so deeply that no one bothered to cross-check the quantity of the items delivered from his store. Meeran resolutely adopted his father's virtues as he ventured with Eastern.

As a young boy, after he completed his schooling, Meeran joined his father to help him run the business and learned the trade. At one point, he felt the need to venture out on his own, either to rubber business at Nilambur or to start a grocery store at Adimali. He finally took the bus to Adimali.

In those days, Adimali was only a stopover for travellers en route to Munnar. Meeran stacked his grocery store with goods sourced from various places. His discipline and systematic management held him in good stead. Vendors were keen to do business with him. The development of Adimali and the growth of Meeran's business happened in tandem. Meeran started distributing Nippo Battery, Kerala Soaps, Mysore Lamps, and Nutrine Chocolates in the Idukki district, making the enterprise more dynamic.

Kochu Madhavan, a close friend of Meeran, the marketing head of Kerala Soaps and Oils, triggered in Meeran an interest in producing his own product. Thus Meeran started the sale of coffee powder in 1982 under the label Eastern Coffee Works. Only later he ventured out with the homemade range of curry powders. The market response to the company's coffee powder was lukewarm compared to the curry powders. Meeran decided against making further investments in coffee, focusing instead on the curry powder business. By 1985, the business flourished beyond Idukki.

One fine morning, Meeran took a landmark decision, one of the many smart moves in the history of the company and Meeran as an entrepreneur. He declared that retailers would no longer be given goods on credit, which no wholesale business person would dare do. But Meeran felt that the business needed more money to expand, so selling on credit was out of the question.

M.E.Meeran and his wife Nabeesa

He was still a distributor for Nestle and Britannia, which gave him a ringside view of the changes in marketing strategies and products. Meeran took note and brought product diversification and new trends in packaging. He introduced Meat Masala, Chicken Masala, Sambar Powder and others, marking Eastern's presence all over Kerala.

Meeran made expansion plans only after personally assessing each business and market trend. It helped him understand business from a close range. It also helped him take corrective measures quickly when required. Even when the business expanded, he was keen on product quality; he did not have to think twice about rejecting substandard products; he never sold them at a lower price. Amidst all these, a modern factory to produce Eastern products came up at Adimali.

Eastern, which triumphed in Kerala, gained popularity in other states as well. By the 1990s, 'Eastern Curry Powder', as heard in the sing-song voice in the popular advertisement jingle, had reached supermarket shelves abroad.

M.E.Meeran receiving Spices Board's Top Exporter Award -2006-07 from
Jairam Ramesh, the then Minister for Trade, Govt.of India

Eastern was a regular winner of the Spices Board Awards for being India's largest exporter of curry powder. The company now has units in Adimali, Theni, Kothamangalam, Perumbavoor and Gundur. Eastern also has a processing unit in Ras Al Khaimah, UAE.

The enthusiastic and dedicated businessman in Meeran expanded beyond curry powders. He kickstarted half a dozen companies under the Eastern Group, including Eastern Mattresses, which manufactures beds and pillows under the brand Sunidra, Eastern Treads for rubberised products, and Eastern Mineral Water, to name a few. Apart from this, the group also runs the educational institution Eastern Public School in Adimali.

M.E. Meeran built a professionally-run business empire worth Rs. 500 Crore that employed 2500 people by the time he passed away in 2011. Eastern's tie-up with American company McCormick is proof of his business foresight. Acquisition of Mohanlal's Taste Buds and setting up a storehouse in the UAE are other great management strokes of Meeran.

In 2020, Norwegian consumer goods maker Orkla, through its wholly owned unit MTR Foods, acquired a majority stake in Eastern Condiments. After the deal, 'Group Meeran' now owns tea brand Eastea, jackfruit flour brand Jackfruit365, property development brand Nanma, mattress brand Sunidra and BSE listed company Eastern Treads.

Meeran's life offers one of the best management lessons available from Kerala's repository of businessmen. The awe-inspiring growth of this curry powder seller from the small town of Adimali to become the largest curry powder manufacturer and exporter in India lies as a precious lesson for business students.

M.E. MEERAN

It takes remarkable effort to be a roaring brand in the face of tough competition. M.E. Meeran built his Eastern Group in such a fashion. Meeran was born to Ibrahim and Fathima of the Manalumpaara family in Nellimattom, a village near Kothamangalam, in 1940. He finished his schooling at St. John's School, Nellimattom. Meeran always had a flair for business as he was exposed to its nitty-gritty from a very young age. In 1964, he moved to Adimali, a town in Idukki, starting a wholesale grocery business. He later moved to the production and distribution of curry powder under the Eastern brand in 1982.

Meeran has received numerous recognitions and awards – the Best Businessman Award of Kerala State Industrial Development Corporation (KSIDC), the Best Industrialist Award of the Kerala Industries Department 2004-2005, Dhanam Businessman of the Year Award, M.G. University's Best Businessman Award, Business Deepika's Businessman of Kerala Award and M.K.K. Nair Memorial Award, to name a few. M.E. Meeran passed away on September 8, 2011.

Nabeesa is his wife, and the couple have four children: Navas Meeran (Chairman, Group Meeran), Feroz Meeran (Managing Director, Group Meeran), Nisa Sakkeer, and Soya Sajith. The in-laws are Shereen Navas, Ayisha Feroz, Zakkeer (Managing Director, Swadeshi Group, Kozhikode), and Anwar Sajith.

21

JACOB'S KINGDOM OF HEAVEN

Decades ago, a section of the Mekkattumana Namboodiri family at Meckavu, Mattancherry, Kochi, embraced Christianity. They made Kizhakkambalam, a suburb 30 km away, their new home, clearing some forest land and raising certain crops for their livelihood. The family was later known as Meckamkunnel. On the 10th of Medam in one Malayalam calendar year, when the harvest festival Vishu is celebrated in Kerala, the family couple, Meckamkunnel Chacko, and Anna were blessed with a baby boy. He was from Anna's tenth pregnancy by when the couple had already lost five newborns.

The family astrologer arrived upon the baby's birth and spread his cowrie shells to forecast the future. "Nothing can be said now," he told them and left, adding that he would be back in a few days. The young mother panicked, thinking about the child's fate, and did not know what to do. The astrologer returned after three weeks to find the baby alive and healthy. Spreading the cowrie shells once again, he said. "I have not seen a horoscope as perfect as this. The boy's fame will spread beyond borders. He will overwhelm enemies."

The parents named the baby Jacob. The little boy had a happy childhood, indulging in small acts of mischief. When he was growing up, the region had sunk into a recession. As Jacob's family was well-off, many people came there seeking work to fetch them a day's wages. The six to seven workers, who can first lay hands on the hoes kept at the house in the morning, would be lucky as they get engaged for the work in the day. Soon workers began to fight for laying their hands on the hoes amid abounding starvation. Little Jacob, worried over their predicament, offered a solution to his father: Provide everyone with a hoe. His father told him that they did not have the money to engage so many workers. There Jacob thought of setting up a factory one day that would employ so many people.

During his school days, no one told him about the importance of education in one's life. So at the age of 20, Jacob finally passed the tenth standard. It was no mean feat those days. Soon after, his family decided to get him married. Eliamma from Irumalaveetil in Kothamangalam became his life partner. While contemplating a source of livelihood, a superintendent's job with the Indian Railways came his way for a monthly salary of Rs.350. But his father was not pleased. He promised Jacob Rs.500 for simply walking around their field every day. There was no need to work so far away from home, his father argued. Jacob gave up his attempts at gainful employment.

And the childhood thought of starting a venture that could provide a few people with a source of income stayed alive in the recesses of his mind. Meanwhile, a Congress leader from the region approached Jacob for a loan of Rs 4000, assuring that it would be returned in four days. Jacob withdrew the money deposited at Pala Central Bank and handed it over to the politician without even telling his father. Days passed by, and Jacob asked the leader several times, but the money was not returned. Finally, he put forth a suggestion to Jacob to take up contract work in partnership. The Congress leader also said that his influence within the party would get them the contracts from the government. Since Jacob had no other option, he agreed.

The first contract that they won was from the Electricity Department for Rs.5,500. It was for laying 18 km of electric lines from Kadamattom to Puthenvelikkara. Jacob cycled several kilometres to the site every day to supervise the work. Being a politician, his partner hardly found the time to join him. Moreover, Jacob had the unenviable task of waiting at his partner's toddy shop every day to pay the workers. When the work was finally completed, they together made a profit of Rs.2,000. But the achievement of employing some people, even for a short period, filled Jacob with enough satisfaction. They won another contract soon to build two bridges at Mulanthuruthy and Thuruthikkara. It was a contract worth Rs.45,000. The number of workers increased in due course. But everything was managed by Jacob as his partner was preoccupied with his political role. By then, M.C. Jacob had risen as a prominent contractor who had the authorities' approval.

M.C.Jacob receiving Government of Kerala's Lifetime Achievement Award from Elamaram Kareem, the then Industries Minister of Kerala

The partnership deal with the local leader soon came to an end. He started trading in areca nuts too. The nuts were peeled, dried, and sent to Kolkata, a venture that could employ many people. But it was seasonal.

Curtains fell on the business when some issues cropped up. Then he tried soap distribution. Soon he realised that these were not his forte. The search for an enterprise that did not require him to give bribes and engage in deception led him to aluminium.

Most of the aluminium factories were located in Tamil Nadu, Karnataka, and Andhra Pradesh. He went to Madurai and Tiruchirapalli to learn the workings of aluminium factories firsthand. He also sought the advice of those working in the field. Some of them guided him to prepare a design and proposal for the aluminium factory. The government gave its approval right away. That was in 1968. The new venture was named after his mother, Anna, as Anna Aluminium.

He hired eight workers in the beginning who were sent to Trichy for undergoing training. It was a time when trained aluminium makers were in great demand. The training was an expensive affair, so the appointments were made after taking deposits from the workers. After they returned, more people were trained in Kizhakkambalam by these hands. Soon the manufacturing of aluminium utensils and pots was started at Kizhakkambalam. Clay pots slowly gave way to aluminium vessels, and Anna Aluminium began to flourish. But the Tamil Nadu lobby did not like this growth. By this time Jacob realised that aluminium utensils manufactured by adding black lead posed health hazards. Until then, like other companies, Anna Aluminium too made utensils from scrap aluminium purchased at lower rates. However profitable, Jacob resolved that he did not want products that kill people in the long run. But shutting down a venture which provided a livelihood for many was out of the question now. While thinking of a remedial measure, he understood that pure aluminium was health-friendly. His enquiries for pure aluminium led him to the Indian Aluminium Company. But it was sold at Rs.5.50 per kilo. This would double the cost of production. Many people told him that it was foolish to buy pure aluminium at twice the rate of scrap aluminium.

M.C.Jacob and his wife Eliamma with family

He understood that the company could produce and sell the utensils in the market at Rs.7 after purchasing aluminium for Rs. 5.50 per kg. Then the company still reaped a profit of Re.1 per kg as the selling price was Rs.8. Jacob decided that he would be content with Re.1 as his profit. Manufacturing started using pure aluminium. As a further blow to Jacob, the Tamil Nadu lobby reduced their price to Rs. 7.50 and later to Rs.7. Selling at that price would mean no profit or loss for Anna Aluminium. The production slowed. The 10 tonnes of aluminium received from the Indian Aluminium Company every month was kept in the godown. This practise went on from 1969 to 1973. Jacob, the entrepreneur, stared at a dead end with the godown filled to capacity and bank debt on the rise. But he was unwilling to do anything betraying his conscience. That was when a power cut was announced in Tamil Nadu, plunging the state's aluminium production into a crisis, resulting in a shortage of aluminium vessels in the market. The price jumped to a whopping Rs.35 per kg. Lady Luck smiled on Jacob in the form of the aluminium that he had stored at a lower price in his godown for years. Production of vessels started again, and Anna Aluminium galloped from profit to profit. The turnover reached Rs.1.50 crore soon.

In 1974, a strike broke out, which, however, was stopped at the court's intervention. Later, Jacob received threats from government officials for not paying them bribes. That threat turned into a sales tax raid. Anna

Aluminium was asked to pay Rs 25,000 in tax arrears. But Jacob, who kept an honest and accurate record of his finances, decided to contest the order. Finally, the case came before the Sales Tax Commissioner and was closed without any penalty. The next crisis came in the form of income tax raids. Here too, no irregularities could be found.

As the company grew, the pay for the employees increased. Yet, a few expressed displeasure. "Isn't the company making a huge profit? Is such a pay hike enough?" they murmured. Hearing this, Jacob arranged a tour for the employees at the company's expense to Tiruchirapalli and Madurai, including a visit to aluminium factories there. It was an eye-opener for many of the staff as they saw people slogging for meagre wages. Jacob's employees realised how blessed they were. Later such trips became a regular feature. Anna Aluminium grew beyond Kerala's borders, diversifying into more sectors.

In 1975, Jacob ventured into the garment industry to create employment for more people. The project was named Kizhakkambalam Textiles as a mark of his deep emotional bond with his hometown. Its acronym 'KITEX' became the brand name. When power looms were sanctioned during the tenure of the Achutha Menon Government, about 500 looms were set up at Ernakulam, Kizhakkambalam, and Kozhikode. Many looms shut down after the government failed to materialize its promises. But Jacob did not close down the textile business that he had started. He braved on even facing a loss. Later, KITEX met with success. Malayalis embraced KITEX lungis with a passion. In 1996, he started an independent company in Kizhakkambalam exclusively for garments. It became another feather in M.C. Jacob's entrepreneurial crown. KITEX Garments went on to become the third-largest manufacturer of infant wear in the world.

By 1976, Jacob had also begun 'Saras' to export spices and market curry powder. The Chakson Pressure Cooker was introduced in the market in 1993. The Scoobee Day bags were also introduced in the market later. Time stood witness to the growth of each of these products as super brands from Kerala. M.C. Jacob passed away on June 5, 2011, having lived life his way - firmly believing that honesty in life and trade would hold one in good stead.

M.C. JACOB

An entrepreneur leaving behind a 'super brand legacy' in multiple sectors is not commonplace. M.C. Jacob has a claim to such a stature. Founder of Anna-Kitex group headquartered at Kizhakkambalam, Ernakulam district, Jacob launched popular brands such as Anna (aluminium), Kitex (apparel), Saras (spices), Chakson (pressure cooker), and Scoobee Day (school bags).

He bagged several awards in his lifetime, including the Central Government's Samman Patra Award and the Vice-President's Udyoga Patra Award. The Government of Kerala honoured him with the Lifetime Achievement Award in 2010 for his comprehensive contribution to the development of the state. He died on June 5, 2011.

He is survived by wife Eliamma, children Somy Varghese, Bobby Jacob, Sabu Jacob, and Biji Santosh, daughters-in-law Minni Bobby and Ranjitha Sabu, and sons-in-law Varghese Kurian and Santosh Mathew Abraham.

ACKNOWLEDGEMENTS

Sajini Sahadevan and InkBoat Creative Studio, for helping to bring out this book in English.

Vinod Nedumudy, for skillfully guiding me through editing.

Don Sebastian and Manoj Thomas, for improving the copy.

Prasanth Nandakumar, Soyesh H., Meera Suresh, K.K.Jayakumar, Sreekanth M.Girinath, and Arun Azhakesan, for helping me think the book through.

Lipson Philip, for being a motivator.

My parents M.A.Rahim and M.Ubaidath, for never saying 'no'.

My wife Nifla Razak, being the pillar that holds my life.

My daughters, Eshal and Duaa, the ultimate de-stress troop.